Cambridge Elements ≡

Elements in Philosophy and Logic

edited by
Bradley Armour-Garb
SUNY Albany

Frederick Kroon
The University of Auckland

TEMPORAL LOGICS

Valentin Goranko
Stockholm University

CAMBRIDGE
UNIVERSITY PRESS

CAMBRIDGE
UNIVERSITY PRESS

Shaftesbury Road, Cambridge CB2 8EA, United Kingdom

One Liberty Plaza, 20th Floor, New York, NY 10006, USA

477 Williamstown Road, Port Melbourne, VIC 3207, Australia

314–321, 3rd Floor, Plot 3, Splendor Forum, Jasola District Centre,
New Delhi – 110025, India

103 Penang Road, #05–06/07, Visioncrest Commercial, Singapore 238467

Cambridge University Press is part of Cambridge University Press & Assessment,
a department of the University of Cambridge.

We share the University's mission to contribute to society through the pursuit of
education, learning and research at the highest international levels of excellence.

www.cambridge.org
Information on this title: www.cambridge.org/9781009170109

DOI: 10.1017/9781009170093

First published 2023

A catalogue record for this publication is available from the British Library.

ISBN 978-1-009-17010-9 Paperback
ISSN 2516-418X (online)
ISSN 2516-4171 (print)

Temporal Logics

Elements in Philosophy and Logic

DOI: 10.1017/9781009170093
First published online: August 2023

Valentin Goranko
Stockholm University

Author for correspondence: Valentin Goranko,
valentin.goranko@philosophy.su.se

Abstract: Temporal logics are a rich variety of logical systems designed for formalising reasoning about time and about events and changes in the world over time. These systems differ by the ontological assumptions made about the nature of time in the associated models, by the logical languages involving various operators for composing temporalised expressions, and by the formal logical semantics adopted for capturing the precise intended meaning of these temporal operators. Temporal logics have found a wide range of applications as formal frameworks for temporal knowledge representation and reasoning in artificial intelligence, and as tools for formal specification, analysis, and verification of properties of computer programs and systems. This Element aims at providing both a panoramic view on the landscape of the variety of temporal logics and closer looks at some of their most interesting and important landmarks.

Keywords: logic, temporal, reasoning, linear time, branching time

ISBNs: (HB), 9781009170109 (PB), 9781009170093 (OC)
ISSNs: 2516-418X (online), 2516-4171 (print)

Contents

Preface

Dear reader,

By reading this Element you are making an eternal mark on the history of the world, both in its past and in its future. Indeed:

i) It has always in the past been the case that you would be reading this Element (sometime in the future of that past).

ii) It will always in the future be the case that you had been reading this Element (sometime in the past of that future).

These two statements are simple, but important, patterns of *temporal reasoning*, which is the subject of this Element. More precisely, the Element is about *temporal logical reasoning* based on various formal systems of *temporal logics*.

This concise exposition is intended to provide some philosophical insights and discussions on the role and applications of formal logic to temporal reasoning, as well as some technical details, including some illustrative proofs, of the semantic and deductive aspects of these applications. It was a challenging task to strike a good balance between these within the space limitations, but I hope that readers interested in either of these aspects of temporal logics will find enough of interest and value in this Element.

Although the exposition is mostly on a basic level, a beneficial reading of the Element still assumes the reader has some background in formal classical logic, as well as in the basics of propositional modal logics, say, within the first chapters of Hodges (2001), Halbach (2010), or Goranko (2016) for classical logic, and of Fitting and Mendelsohn (1998), Blackburn, de Rijke, and Venema (2001), van Benthem (2010), and Uckelman (in press), on modal logic.

Due to space limitations, I have made few references to the vast relevant literature on temporal logics throughout this Element. This is partly compensated for by the additional references at the end of each section. In addition, key general references on philosophical and technical aspects of temporal logics and on their applications include: Prior (1957, 1967, 1968), Rescher and Urquhart (1971), McArthur (1976), van Benthem (1983), Gabbay, Hodkinson, and Reynolds (1994), van Benthem (1995), Øhrstrøm and Hasle (1995), Gabbay, Reynolds, and Finger (2000), Venema (2001), all chapters in Gabbay and Guenthner (2002), Fisher, Gabbay, and Vila (2005), Demri, Goranko, and Lange (2016), Goranko and Rumberg (2020), and the bibliographies therein.

The undefined notation used in this Element is assumed common or self-explanatory, including the use of $\mathbb{N}, \mathbb{Z}, \mathbb{Q}, \mathbb{R}$ to denote, respectively, the sets of natural numbers, integers, rationals, and reals.

1 Temporal Reasoning and Logics: Introduction and a Brief Historical Overview

What is temporal logic? This is the first question that springs to mind for the uninitiated reader seeing this Element. While the Element itself aims to give the ultimate answer, I will begin with a very brief and sketchy historical overview on temporal reasoning and the origins of temporal logic.

1.1 What Is Time?

Temporal logics are logics for *reasoning about Time*. So, the question to ask before looking further is *what is Time*? A classic quote by Augustine of Hippo (aka Saint Augustine, AD 354-430) says:

> *What then is time?*
> *If no one asks me, I know what it is.*
> *If I wish to explain it to him who asks, I do not know.*

I am afraid we are not much wiser today on that question. Indeed, various witty, but mostly superficial, answers have been proposed, such as:

> *Time is nature's way to keep everything from happening all at once.*

> *Time is the sequence of the events happening in the universe.*

or just:

> *Time is what clocks measure.*

None of these are really satisfactory, especially after the insights on the relativity of time that have come from twentieth-century physics and cosmology. Apparently, understanding time takes time .... So, I will simply take it as a primitive concept on which the reader has some initial intuition. That intuition will be refined, enriched, and also challenged in this Element.

1.2 What Is Temporal Logic?

This is a much easier question. The most concise answer is that, whereas classical logic reasons about a snapshot of the universe, where everything is fixed (also in truth value), temporal logic reasons about the temporal dynamics of the universe, that is, about what is happening as time passes and how that affects the truth of propositions about the world. Thus, temporal logic is not so much about reasoning *about time*, but rather about reasoning about events happening *in time*. More precisely, temporal logic helps us formalise and conduct reasoning with *temporal propositions*, such as the following:

- You are reading (*now*).
- *Sometime in the past* you were not reading.
- Sometime in the future you will not be reading.
- You will be reading *sometime in the future* and *never in the future* thereafter.
- *Always in the past* you were going to be reading (*sometime in the future of that past*).
- *Always (in the future)* you will have been reading (*in the past of that future*).
- It will (*sometime in the future*) be the case that you have been reading (*for a while*) but that you are not reading *any more*.
- *Sometime in the past* you were not reading but it had *always before* been the case that you were going to be reading (*sometime in the future of that past*).
- You have been reading *since sometime in the past* and will go on reading *until sometime in the future*, and so on.

Suppose you are wondering, for instance, whether

> the fact that *you are reading this book now, but were not reading it a year ago, logically implies that you have been reading the book since sometime in the past when you had never been reading it before, but you would be reading it until some future time when you will not be reading it ever again.*

Then, you are doing the kind of temporal logical reasoning which this Element is about. And, if you wish to know the answer, it is: *it depends*! It depends on some ontological assumptions about the nature of time, on the formal logical language used, and how exactly the query above is formalised in it, as well as on the precise, formal logical semantics which you adopt for defining the notion of logical consequence to which that query refers. So, in fact, as we will see further, there is not just one and only one *temporal logic* that covers all our temporal logical reasoning, but a rich variety of many systems of *temporal logics*, suited for reasoning under different assumptions, in different formal languages, and for different formal semantics adopted for them. This Element aims at providing a panoramic view on the landscape of these temporal logics.

1.3 Origins and Antiquity: Zeno's Paradoxes and Sea-Battles

Temporal reasoning has been an essential aspect of human reasoning ever since humans developed the concept of time. While we do not seem to know when exactly that happened, the discussion on temporality and reasoning about time goes back to antiquity, and examples can be found even in the Bible. Then, in Ancient Greece we find Zeno's arguments referring to the apparently paradoxical nature of time manifested by the infinite divisibility of time (and space) intervals. Zeno's paradoxes 'The Dichotomy', 'Achilles and the

Tortoise', and 'The Arrow' challenge our concept of time and its properties, and the closely related notions of space, motion, and change.

Perhaps the earliest more explicit reference to logical aspects of temporal reasoning, however, is Aristotle's argument in *De Interpretatione* Aristotle (1984/350, ch. 9) that definite truth-values cannot, at the present time, be ascribed to *future contingents*, that is, to statements about future events which may or may not occur, such as '*There will be a sea-battle tomorrow.*'

1.4 Time, Necessity, and Determinism: Diodorus Cronus' Master Argument

Just a few decades after Aristotle, the philosopher Diodorus Cronus from the Megarian school demonstrated the problem with future contingents in his famous Master Argument, based on the following three propositions:

(D1) *Every proposition which is true about the past is necessarily true.*
(D2) *An impossible proposition cannot follow[1] from a possible one.*
(D3) *There is a proposition which is possible, but which neither is, nor will be true.*

Diodorus argued[2] that these cannot all be true together, yet (D1) and (D2) should be accepted as true. Consequently, (D3) must be rejected. Therefore, 'possible' can be defined as '*that which is true or will ever become true*' and, correspondingly, 'necessary' is '*that which is true and will always be true*'. Diodorus' argument has been regarded as supporting determinism, even fatalism.

I will come back to the Master Argument in Section 5, where I will present Prior's formal reconstruction of that argument and his proposed formal logical solutions leading to the birth of logics of branching time.

1.5 Medieval Times: Determinism versus Free Will

During the Middle Ages there were heated philosophical and theological debates on free will vs. determinism. The problem at the heart of these debates was how to reconcile God's foreknowledge of a person's future decisions and actions, suggesting that the evolution of the world is predetermined, with the that person's free will and moral accountability for their decisions and actions.

---

[1] Note the possible ambiguity: 'follow' can be read in a temporal or in a logical sense. Apparently, Diodorus meant the latter, in the sense of Lewis' strict implication.

[2] Unfortunately, the original version of the argument itself has not been preserved.

Notably, the thirteenth-century scholastic philosopher and theologian William of Ockham held that propositions about the contingent future cannot be known in advance by humans as true or false, but *humans have a freedom of choice between different possible futures, even though God – being independent of time and beyond it – already knows that possible future that will actually take place.* This position suggests the idea of a *tree-like, forward-branching model of time*, where the past is fixed and cannot be changed, but there are many possible futures, hence many timelines (histories), of which just one will *actually* take place (the idea of the 'Thin Red Line', which can also be traced in the works of the sixteenth-century Jesuit priest and scholar Luis de Molina). Furthermore, the truth of statements about the future is relativised to the possible future that is presumed to be the actual one. This model of time, now often called *Ockhamist*, gives rise to Prior's *Ockhamist semantics* of branching time logic, presented in Section 7.

Another landmark in the medieval history of temporal logic is Avicenna's (Ibn Sina's) extension of Aristotle's syllogisms with temporal aspects, such as 'All A are always B', 'All A are at some time B', 'Some A are never B', and so on.

1.6 Precursors to Temporal Logic

Various arguments and patterns of reasoning about temporality, related to non-determinism, historical necessity, humans' free will, God's will and knowledge, and so on, were proposed in post-medieval times and until the twentieth century. Some such temporal arguments can be found, inter alia, in the works of Boole, Hamilton, Bergson, and most notably Peirce, who disagreed with the view, prevailing then amongst philosophers, that time is an 'extra-logical matter' and argued in favour of logic-based treatment of time and temporality. However, Peirce objected to the idea that future contingents can currently have definite truth values, as he argued that there is no '*actual future*' yet at present, but only many such *possible futures*. Therefore, according to him, truth in the future should mean truth in *all* possible futures. Later, his ideas led Prior to introduce one of his main systems of branching time temporal logics which he called 'Peircean', presented in Section 6.

Much more happened in philosophy and other sciences during the early-mid twentieth century which paved the way to the emergence of formal temporal logic. Here are some landmarks:

- In 1908, Hermann Minkowski gave a public lecture on 'Space and Time' where he presented the ideas of relativity of time and its close relationship with space, eventually leading to what is now called '*Minkowski's*

4-dimensional spacetime'. Later in the twentieth century, several formal logical systems were developed, purporting to formalise and axiomatise Minkowski's spacetime.

- Again in 1908, John McTaggart, driven by the idea to demonstrate the 'unreality of time', proposed two alternative approaches to modelling time, now known as *McTaggart's time series*. See Section 3.4 on these and their relation with formal logical reasoning about time.

- In 1920, motivated by attempts to resolve Aristotle's 'sea-battle tomorrow' puzzle and the related problems with future contingents, Jan Łukasiewicz proposed a *three-valued logic*, assigning to future contingent statements the new, third truth value of 'undetermined'.

- In 1947, Hans Reichenbach, following some ideas of Otto Jespersen, developed his very influential *theory of tenses*, where he characterised most of the tenses in natural language by using a triple of time points related to the utterance of tensed statements, namely: the *speech time* S, the *reference time* R, and the *event time* E. For more on that, see Section 9.5.3 and the bibliographic notes.

- Again in 1947, Jerzy Łoś presented a 'positional calculus' intended to formalise 'Mill's canons', in which he used certain temporal functions. His system is regarded by some as one of the prime precursors of modern temporal logic.

- Several other twentieth-century philosophers, including Bertrand Russell, John Findlay, and Charles Hamblin, have also provided important insights leading to the creation of temporal logic; see some references at the end of this section.

1.7 The Birth of Temporal Logic: Prior and Post-Prior

In the 1940s the philosopher and logician Arthur Prior became strongly interested in philosophical and theological problems related to determinism and divine foreknowledge versus indeterminism, human free will, and moral responsibility. In that context, Prior set out to analyse, formalise, and eventually try to resolve some famous problems and arguments from antiquity, including Aristotle's 'sea-battle tomorrow' problem and Diodorus Cronus' Master Argument. Besides, he also wanted to develop a logical theory of tenses. That led him to the invention of several formal systems of what he then called 'tense logic', several of which are presented and discussed here. As acknowledged by himself, Prior's seminal work was influenced by some important precursors mentioned earlier, including Findlay (whom Prior regarded as the founding father of temporal logic), Reichenbach, Łukasiewicz, and Łoś. Prior's work initiated the modern epoch of temporal logical reasoning, which found numerous important applications not only in philosophy, but also in computer science, artificial intelligence, and linguistics, briefly discussed in Section 9.5.

Some References

For further readings on the history of temporal reasoning and logics see Prior (1957), Prior (1967), Rescher and Urquhart (1971, ch. XVII), Øhrstrøm and Hasle (1995), Øhrstrøm and Hasle (2006), Meyer (2013), Meyer (2015), Hodges and Johnston (2017), Øhrstrøm (2019), Øhrstrøm and Hasle (2020). For more on Prior's philosophical views on time, see also Hasle, Blackburn, and Øhrstrøm (2017), Blackburn, Hasle, and Øhrstrøm (2019).

2 The Variety of Models of Time

What is the right model of the flow of time? Is it unique, or are there many? What properties does time have? Is it discrete or dense, continuous or gappy? Is it linear, or branching into the future? Does time have a beginning or an end? Or is it not circular, as our watches and calendars suggest? Further, what are the primitive entities in the structure of time – time instants, or time intervals, or something else?

These fundamental ontological and philosophical questions about the nature of time do not have definitive and unique answers, but they rather lead to a rich variety of formal models of time, and respectively to a variety of temporal logics, including *logics for linear time and for branching time, logics for discrete time and for dense time, point-based logics and interval-based logics*, and so on. Before exploring these logics, let us first look at the two most basic types of formal models of time with respect to the temporal entities which they adopt as primitives: *instant-based* and *interval-based* models.

2.1 Instant-Based Models of Time and Their Properties

The primitive entities in instant-based models of time are *points in time*, usually called **(time) instants**, or **moments**. The basic relationship between them, besides equality, is **temporal precedence**. Thus, an **instant-based model of time** is a structure of the type $\mathcal{T} = \langle T, < \rangle$, consisting of a non-empty set of instants T with a binary relation $<$ of precedence on it. Sometimes, the preference relation will be given as $\leq$, where $x \leq y$ is an abbreviation of $x < y \lor x = y$. If $s, t \in \mathcal{T}$ and $s < t$, then we say that s **precedes** t, or that s **is a predecessor of** t, and respectively that t **succeeds** s, or t **is a successor of** s.

Some natural properties can be imposed on the precedence relation in instant-based models of time. Most (but not all) such properties can be expressed by sentences of classical first-order logic for instant-based models, as follows:

- **reflexivity** (every instant precedes itself): $\forall x(x < x)$.
- **irreflexivity** (no instant precedes itself): $\forall x \neg(x < x)$.
  I hereafter assume that $<$ is irreflexive,[3] unless otherwise stated.
- **transitivity**: $\forall x \forall y \forall z(x < y \land y < z \rightarrow x < z)$.
  An irreflexive and transitive relation is called a **strict partial ordering**. A reflexive and transitive relation is called a **(non-strict) partial pre-ordering**.
- **asymmetry** (two instants cannot precede each other):
  $\forall x \forall y \neg(x < y \land y < x)$.
  Note that every strict partial ordering is asymmetric.
- **anti-symmetry** (if two instants precede each other, then they are identical):
  $\forall x \forall y(x < y \land y < x \rightarrow x = y)$.
  An anti-symmetric partial pre-ordering is called a **partial ordering**.
- **trichotomy** (every two instants are *comparable*, i.e., they are either identical, or one precedes the other): $\forall x \forall y(x = y \lor x < y \lor y < x)$.
  This property is also known as **connectedness**, or **linearity**.
  A strict (respectively, non-strict) partial ordering which satisfies trichotomy is a **strict linear ordering** (respectively, **non-strict linear ordering**).
- **forward-connectedness**, aka **forward-linearity** (every two instants which are preceded by the same instant are comparable):
  $\forall x \forall y \forall z(z < x \land z < y \rightarrow (x = y \lor x < y \lor y < x))$.
- **backward-connectedness**, aka **backward-linearity** (every two instants which precede the same instant are comparable):
  $\forall x \forall y \forall z(x < z \land y < z \rightarrow (x = y \lor x < y \lor y < x))$.
- **existence of a beginning**: $\exists x \neg \exists y(y < x)$.
- **existence of an end**: $\exists x \neg \exists y(x < y)$.
- **no beginning**: $\forall x \exists y(y < x)$.
- **no end (unboundedness)**: $\forall x \exists y(x < y)$.
- **density** (between every two instants, of which one precedes the other, there is an instant): $\forall x \forall y(x < y \rightarrow \exists z(x < z \land z < y))$;
- **forward-discreteness** (every non-last instant has an immediate successor):
  $\forall x \forall y(x < y \rightarrow \exists z(x < z \land z \leq y \land \neg \exists u(x < u \land u < z)))$;

---

[3] This is not an ontological assumption, just a matter of convention on the time precedence.

- **backward-discreteness** (every non-first instant has an immediate predecessor): $\forall x \forall y (y < x \rightarrow \exists z(z < x \wedge y \leq z \wedge \neg \exists u(z < u \wedge u < x)))$.

A (instant-based) model of time $\mathcal{T} = \langle T, < \rangle$, is (strictly) **linear** if $<$ is a (strict) linear ordering.

Note that, in linear models, the two discreteness conditions simplify to

- $\forall x \forall y (x < y \rightarrow \exists z(x < z \wedge \forall u(x < u \rightarrow z \leq u)))$ and, respectively:
- $\forall x \forall y (y < x \rightarrow \exists z(z < x \wedge \forall u(u < x \rightarrow u \leq z)))$.

A model of time $\mathcal{T} = \langle T, < \rangle$, is **tree-like**, or **forward-branching** if $<$ is a backward-linear partial ordering, that is, a partial ordering in which every instant has the set of its predecessors ordered by $<$.

Linear and forward-branching models are the two most common types of instant-based models of time, where the former capture the view that time (or, the world) is deterministic, whereas the latter represent the view that only the past is deterministic and has no alternatives, where as the future is not deterministic but branches into many alternative possible futures. Both views are natural and meaningful, and each of them provides semantics for a family of temporal logics. These will be discussed respectively in Sections 4 and 5.

Another important distinction is between *discrete* and *dense*, or even *continuous* models of time. The former are typically used in artificial intelligence and in computer science, where the flow of time represents a discrete succession of events, transitions, or stages of a computational process. The latter usually represent 'real, physical time' and are more common in natural sciences.

There are examples of natural properties of instant-based models of time that cannot be expressed by first-order sentences, but require an essentially *second-order* logical language, with quantification not only over individual instants, but also over *sets of instants*. Some of the most important such examples are *Dedekind completeness, continuity, well-ordering, forward/backward induction*, and the *finite interval property*. I will informally describe these in linear models.

- **Dedekind completeness** means that every non-empty set of elements that is bounded above has a least upper bound. Examples are the ordered sets of the natural numbers, integers, and real numbers; while a non-example is the ordering of the rational numbers: for instance, the set of all rational numbers whose square is less than 2 is bounded above (say, by 2) but its least upper bound is $\sqrt{2}$, which is not a rational number.
- The property of **continuity** means that there are no 'gaps' in the precedence order. To be continuous, the temporal order must be both dense and Dedekind complete. Thus, the orderings of the natural numbers and of the integers are not continuous, but the ordering of the reals is.

- A linear instant-based model is **well ordered** if every non-empty set of instants has a least element. Equivalently, if there are no infinite (strictly) descending sequences of instants. Well-ordering is closely related (in a sense, even equivalent) to the **principle of transfinite induction** generalising the usual mathematical induction on natural numbers.

- A partial ordering is **forward inductive** if every infinite <-ascending sequence of instants is **co-final**, meaning that every instant precedes some instant in the sequence. In other words, such a sequence has no *strict upper bound*, and hence there are no 'transfinite instants' in the future. Respectively, it is **backward inductive**, if every infinite <-descending sequence of instants is **co-initial**, meaning that every instant succeeds some instant in the sequence, so such a sequence has no *strict lower bound*. Thus, every well-ordered model is vacuously backward inductive. A non-trivial example is the ordering of the integers, which is both backward and forward inductive, but it is not well ordered. No dense ordering is either backward or forward inductive; however, non-density is not sufficient to ensure either of these. For instance, extend the ordering of the natural numbers with an 'infinite number' ∞, greater than any of them. Then the sequence of all natural numbers is not co-final, as ∞ does not precede any of them, hence the resulting ordering is not forward inductive.

- Lastly, a linear model has the **finite interval property** if between any two elements there are only finitely many instants. This is the case precisely when it is both backward and forward inductive. Note that this property is incomparable with well-ordering. For example: the natural numbers are both well ordered and have the finite interval property; the integers (or, the negative integers) are not well ordered but still have the finite interval property; any transfinite ordinal (e.g., $\omega + 1$, the natural numbers extended with ∞), is well ordered but does not have the finite interval property; and the positive reals are neither well ordered nor do they have the finite interval property.

We will see in Section 3.6 that each of these properties can be expressed in a precise sense by means of propositional temporal formulae.

2.2 Interval-Based Models of Time

Instant-based models of time are often not suitable for reasoning about events with duration. To represent such events, one should rather use models with underlying temporal ontology based on *time intervals*, that is, time periods rather than time instants, as the primitive entities. The roots of interval-based temporal reasoning can be traced back to Zeno and Aristotle. Apparently, Zeno

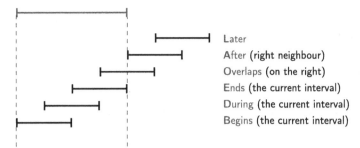

Figure 1 The thirteen relations between two time intervals on a linear ordering: the six listed relations, their inverses, and the identity relation.

himself noticed that some of his paradoxes do not arise in an interval-based setting, for example the *flying arrow paradox* (if at each *instant* the flying arrow stands still, how is movement possible?) and the *dividing instant dilemma* (if the light is on and it is turned off, what is its state at the *instant* between the two events?). And, there are many examples of natural language statements that naturally require interval-based, or combined instant-interval based reasoning, for example: '*While explaining the proof to the students, the professor found a mistake in it*', '*Some students kept dozing off and waking up during the lecture, while others slept through it*', '*Joe had been thinking for a while when Mia came, and then he started drinking and kept drinking until she left, right after which he passed out*', and so on.

Interval-based models are usually based on linear time flows. Still, they are ontologically much richer than instant-based linear models, as there are many more possible temporal relations between time intervals than between time instants. Indeed, while there are only three possible relations between two instants on a linear order (the one can be *earlier than*, can *coincide with*, or can be *later than* the other), it is quite easy to observe that there are twelve other possible relations, besides the identity, that can arise between two intervals in a linear order. These were first studied systematically in Allen (1983), who also pointed out their use in temporal representation and reasoning in AI, and they were subsequently called *Allen's relations*. These thirteen binary relations, displayed in the table in Figure 1, are mutually exclusive and jointly exhaustive, that is, exactly one of them holds between any given pair of *proper* intervals (excluding point-intervals).

Thus, there are a variety of $2^{12} - 1 = 4,095$ non-trivial types of interval-based models of time, depending on which of these relations are taken as primitives. For example, one such type includes the relations of interval *precedence* $\prec$, *inclusion* $\sqsubseteq$, and *overlap* O, over a set of intervals T on some linear order. Formally, these models are of the type $\mathcal{T} = \langle T, \prec, \sqsubseteq, O \rangle$. Some natural properties of the relations in such interval-based models include:

- *reflexivity of* $\sqsubseteq$: $\forall x(x \sqsubseteq x)$;
- *anti-symmetry of* $\sqsubseteq$: $\forall x \forall y(x \sqsubseteq y \land y \sqsubseteq x \rightarrow x = y)$;
- *atomicity of* $\sqsubseteq$ (for discrete time): $\forall x \exists y(y \sqsubseteq x \land \forall z(z \sqsubseteq y \rightarrow z = y))$;
- *downward monotonicity of* $\prec$ *w.r.t.* $\sqsubseteq$: $\forall x \forall y \forall z(x \prec y \land z \sqsubseteq x \rightarrow z \prec y)$;
- *symmetry of* O: $\forall x \forall y(xOy \rightarrow yOx)$;
- *overlapping intervals intersect in a subinterval:*
  $\forall x \forall y(xOy \rightarrow \exists z(z \sqsubseteq x \land z \sqsubseteq y \land \forall u(u \sqsubseteq x \land u \sqsubseteq y \rightarrow u \sqsubseteq z)))$;
- *monotonicity of* $\sqsubseteq$ *w.r.t.* O: $\forall x \forall y \forall z(x \sqsubseteq y \land xOz \rightarrow z \sqsubseteq y \lor zOy)$, and so on.

Given an abstract *interval structure* defined by a certain set of interval relations of arbitrary arity required to satisfy certain properties, the question arises whether it can be represented by means of a concrete interval-based structure over linear time. Answers are provided by *representation theorems*; see some references at the end of this Section.

2.3 Instant-Based versus Interval-Based Models of Time

The choice between instants and intervals as the primary objects of temporal ontology has been a much-debated philosophical theme since the times of Zeno and Aristotle. Technically, the two types of temporal ontologies are interreducible: on the one hand, time intervals can be defined by pairs of time instants (beginning and end); on the other hand, a time instant can be construed as a *point-interval*, whose beginning and end points coincide. Still, these technical reductions do not resolve the semantic question of whether sentences are to be evaluated with respect to instants or with respect to intervals, and one may argue that both instants and intervals are needed as mutually complementary. Thus, the idea of *two-sorted point-interval models* emerges. More complex models of time have also been proposed and studied, including models of *time granularity* which allow for different resolution levels of temporal intervals (e.g., minutes, hours, days, years, etc.), as well as *metric and layered temporal models*, and so on.

In Section 9.1, I briefly discuss a variety of interval-based temporal logics, especially those arising by associating modal operators with Allen's relations.

Some References

For further reading on temporal ontologies and models of time see Walker (1947), Hamblin (1972), Kamp (1979), Humberstone (1979), van Benthem (1983), Moszkowski (1983), Ladkin (1987), Venema (1990), Venema (1991), McCall (1994), Øhrstrøm and Hasle (1995), Galton (1996), Montanari (1996), Euzenat and Montanari (2005), Øhrstrøm and Hasle (2006), Dyke and Bardon (2013), Meyer (2013), and Emery, Markosian, and Sullivan (2020).

3 Prior's Basic Systems of Temporal Logic

The first formal systems of 'tense logic' were introduced by Arthur Prior in Prior (1957), later refined and extended in Prior (1967) and Prior (1968). Prior's motivation for inventing tense logic was mostly philosophical, though his ideas were also strongly inspired by the use of tenses in natural language. Prior's key idea was to treat propositions as tensed, rather than tenseless, as they are in classical logic. Formally, this was achieved by the introduction of *temporal operators* into the language, which are treated as modal operators. Prior himself referred to his tensed logical system as *tense logic*, whereas gradually the terminology changed to the more generic expression *temporal logic*.[4]

3.1 Prior's Tense Operators

Prior built his basic tense logic in the style of a propositional modal logic, but instead of modal operators he used the following four simple tense operators:

P: '*It has at some past time been the case that ...*'
F: '*It will at some future time be the case that ...*'
H: '*It has always in the past been the case that ...*'
G: '*It will always in the future be the case that ...*'

For example, let ϕ be the proposition '*A man walks on the moon*'. Then Pϕ means to say '*It has at some past time been the case (or, it was true) that a man walks on the moon*', that is, '*Sometime in the past a man walked on the moon*'. Respectively, GPϕ means '*Always in the future, sometime in the past (of that future) a man will have walked on the moon*', and so on.[5]

Prior's tense logic TL involves one pair of temporal operators for the past, P and H, and one pair of temporal operators for the future, F and G. The operators P and F are often referred to as the *weak* temporal operators, while H and G are known as the *strong* ones.

The set of formulae of TL can be inductively defined over a given set of atomic propositions PROP by the following formal grammar:

$$\varphi := p \in \text{PROP} \mid \bot \mid \neg\varphi \mid (\varphi \wedge \varphi) \mid P\varphi \mid F\varphi.$$

---

[4] In this Element I will distinguish these two terms and will use them both, but in somewhat different senses. The term 'temporal logic' will be used generically, also in plural, to refer to various tensed logical systems.

[5] Using phrases like 'it is/was/will be the case' or 'it is/was/will be true' sometimes sounds a little awkward and they will usually be omitted hereafter, but they are quite handy for a more precise translation of expressions with nested temporal operators, as in 'Always in the future it will be the case (or, true) that at sometime in the past it was the case (or, true) that a man walked on the moon.'

The other truth-functional connectives $\vee, \rightarrow$, and $\leftrightarrow$ are definable in terms of $\neg$ and $\wedge$ as usual. The strong past and future operators are now defined[6] as respective duals of P and F:

$$H\varphi := \neg P\neg\varphi \text{ and } G\varphi \equiv \neg F\neg\varphi.$$

Besides, we define the operator **Always** as $A\varphi = H\varphi \wedge \varphi \wedge G\varphi$ and, dually, **Sometime** as $E\varphi = P\varphi \vee \varphi \vee F\varphi$. Indeed, on linear models of time these mean 'always' and 'sometime', respectively.

Prior's introduction of the temporal operators was initially motivated by the use of tenses in natural language. Various tensed expressions in natural language can, at least approximately, be captured in TL. For example:

$P\varphi$: 'φ *was* the case' or 'φ *has been* the case'.

$F\varphi$: 'φ *will be* the case'.

$PP\varphi$: 'φ *had been* the case'.

$FP\varphi$: 'φ *will have been* the case'.

$PF\varphi$: 'φ *would be* the case' or 'φ *was going to be* the case'.

$PFP\varphi$: 'φ *would have been* the case' or 'φ *was going to have been* the case'.

These examples lead to the abstract notion of a **tense**, defined as any (possibly empty) string $X_1, \ldots X_n$ of temporal operators from $\{F, P, G, H\}$. Examples: all of the above, as well as the empty string (for *now*), GPF, FGFGHHPGGF, and so on. Also, some natural temporal expressions are now formalised with tenses, like:

$FG\varphi$, often denoted as $G^\infty\varphi$: 'φ *holds eventually always*',

$GF\varphi$, often denoted as $F^\infty\varphi$: 'φ *repeats infinitely often*'[7] (if the precedence is irreflexive and time has no end).

In a given temporal logic, some tenses may turn out equivalent, in a sense of generating logically equivalent formulae, for example, F, FF, FFF, and so on in any logic where $Gq \equiv GGq$ is a valid equivalence. Notably, Hamblin (later also joined by Prior), identified exactly fifteen different such tenses that can be expressed in TL on the time flow of the rational numbers $(\mathbb{Q}, \leq)$ (i.e., reflexive and dense linear order without endpoints), where they showed that any sequence of temporal operators reduces to a sequence of at most two operators.

Still, Prior's operators are not suitable for expressing *progressive* (aka, continuous) *tenses*. Arguably, interval-based logic is a more natural framework for that. For examples and more on that issue, see Sections 2.2 and 9.1.

---

[6] The choice of the weak operators as primitives is made only for historical reasons, following Prior. Instead, the strong operators G and H can be taken as primitives and the weak ones as definable, and that would have some technical advantage in the axiomatisations.

[7] This is a somewhat weaker reading. For instance, if φ is true at every real point in the interval $[0,1]$, then it does repeat infinitely often, but $GF\varphi$ is not true at 0 in the time frame of real numbers.

3.2 Semantics of TL

The standard semantics of TL is essentially a *possible worlds semantics*, familiar from modal logic. It is often also called *Kripke semantics*, though Prior apparently introduced it in the context of tense logics a couple of years before Kripke's seminal 1963 papers. In modal logic, propositional formulae are evaluated in so-called *Kripke models* consisting of a non-empty set of possible worlds, an accessibility relation between them, and a valuation of the atomic propositions into sets of possible worlds where they are declared true. In temporal logics, the possible worlds are time instants and the accessibility relation has a concrete interpretation in terms of temporal precedence. In other words, the truth of formulae of TL is evaluated at instants in an instant-based model of time $\mathcal{T} = \langle T, < \rangle$, hereafter also called a **tense frame**. Note that so far no conditions, like transitivity, reflexivity, or irreflexivity are imposed on the precedence relation $<$. A tense frame $\langle T, < \rangle$ in which $<$ is transitive will be called a **temporal frame**.

Given a fixed set of atomic propositions PROP, a **tense model** (respectively, **temporal model**) for TL is a triple $\mathcal{M} = \langle T, <, V \rangle$ where $\mathcal{T} = \langle T, < \rangle$ is a tense frame (respectively, temporal frame) and V is a **valuation** assigning to each atomic proposition $p \in$ PROP the set of instants $V(p) \subseteq T$ at which p is considered true. Alternatively, the truth of the atomic propositions can be specified by a function $I : T \times \text{PROP} \rightarrow \{true, false\}$, which assigns a truth value to each atomic proposition at each instant in the temporal frame[8], or by a **labelling**, or **state description function** $L : T \rightarrow \mathcal{P}(\text{PROP})$, which assigns to each instant the set of atomic propositions that are considered true at that instant. Clearly, all these types of structures are inter-definable, so hereafter I will use whichever one is more convenient for the current purpose. The **truth of a formula** φ **of** TL **at an instant** t **in a given tense model** $\mathcal{M}$ (denoted $\mathcal{M}, t \models \varphi$) is then defined recursively as follows:

- $\mathcal{M}, t \models p$ iff $t \in V(p)$, for $p \in$ PROP;
- $\mathcal{M}, t \not\models \bot$ (that is, it is not the case that $\mathcal{M}, t \models \bot$);
- $\mathcal{M}, t \models \neg \varphi$ iff $\mathcal{M}, t \not\models \varphi$;
- $\mathcal{M}, t \models \varphi \wedge \psi$ iff $\mathcal{M}, t \models \varphi$ and $\mathcal{M}, t \models \psi$;
- $\mathcal{M}, t \models \mathsf{P}\varphi$ iff $\mathcal{M}, s \models \varphi$ for some earlier instant s, that is, such that $s < t$;
- $\mathcal{M}, t \models \mathsf{F}\varphi$ iff $\mathcal{M}, s \models \varphi$ for some later instant s, that is, such that $t < s$.

Consequently, for the duals H and G, it holds that:

- $\mathcal{M}, t \models \mathsf{H}\varphi$ iff $\mathcal{M}, s \models \varphi$ for all earlier instants s, that is, such that $s < t$;
- $\mathcal{M}, t \models \mathsf{G}\varphi$ iff $\mathcal{M}, s \models \varphi$ for all later instants s, that is, such that $t < s$.

---

[8] This function-based version allows one to consider many-valued underlying logics, with truth values such as true, false, neither, both.

Note that, from the point of view of modal logic, there are (formally speaking) two different accessibility relations involved here: an 'earlier-relation' in the case of the past operators and a 'later-relation' in the case of the future operators. In the context of temporal logic these two relations are uniformly captured by a single precedence relation; after all, 'earlier' and 'later' are just converses of each other (i.e., t is earlier than t' iff t' is later than t).

Now, here are the basic semantic notions, derivative from the truth definition that apply, *mutatis mutandis*, to every temporal logical system introduced hereafter. A formula φ of TL is: **valid in a tense model** $\mathcal{M}$, denoted $\mathcal{M} \models \varphi$, if it is true at every instant in that model; **valid in a temporal frame** $\mathcal{T}$, denoted $\mathcal{T} \models \varphi$, if it is valid in every model on that frame; **valid**, denoted $\models \varphi$, if it is valid in all temporal frames, that is, true at every instant in every tense model; **satisfiable**, if its negation is not valid, that is, if φ is true at some instant in some tense model. A **formula φ follows logically from a set** Γ **of formulae**, or Γ **logically implies** φ, denoted $\Gamma \models \varphi$, if φ is true at every instant in every model where each formula of Γ is true.

3.3 Standard Translation of TL into First-Order Logic

Let $\mathrm{PROP} = \{p_0, p_1, \ldots\}$ be the (fixed) set of atomic propositions of TL, and let L_1 be a first-order language with $=$, a binary predicate symbol R, and a denumerable set of unary predicate symbols $\mathcal{P} = \{P_0, P_1, \ldots\}$, one for each atomic proposition in PROP. We also fix an enumeration $\{x_0, x_1, \ldots\}$ of the set VAR of individual variables of L_1. We define a **standard translation** ST of the formulae of TL into L_1 as follows, where $x \in \mathrm{VAR}$ and $\theta[y/x]$ is the result of substituting y for each free occurrence of x in θ:

- $ST(p_i) = P_i(x); \quad ST(\bot) = \bot;$
- $ST(\neg\varphi) = \neg ST(\varphi); \quad ST(\varphi \wedge \psi) = ST(\varphi) \wedge ST(\psi);$
- $ST(\mathsf{P}\varphi) = \exists y(yRx \wedge ST(\varphi)[y/x])$, where y is a fresh variable;
- $ST(\mathsf{F}\varphi) = \exists y(xRy \wedge ST(\varphi)[y/x])$, where y is a fresh variable.

It then follows that:

$$ST(\mathsf{H}\varphi) = \forall y(yRx \to ST(\varphi)[y/x]); \quad ST(\mathsf{G}\varphi) = \forall y(xRy \to ST(\varphi)[y/x]).$$

For example:

$$ST(\mathsf{G}p_1 \vee \mathsf{F}\mathsf{H}p_2) = \forall y(xRy \to P_1 y) \vee \exists y(xRy \wedge \forall z(zRy \to P_2 z)).$$

Remark. With a little extra care, the individual variables can be reused in the standard translation, so that TL can be translated in the *two-variable fragment* FO^2 of first-order logic (FOL). That, in turn, implies decidability of validity in TL, because validity in FO^2 is decidable, see Grädel and Otto (1999). For instance, the example above can be rewritten as

$ST(\mathsf{G}p_1 \vee \mathsf{FH}p_2) = \forall y(xRy \rightarrow P_1y) \vee \exists y(xRy \wedge \forall x(xRy \rightarrow P_2x))$.

The standard translation of TL into FOL enables a systematic treatment of various technical aspects of temporal logic with the tools and techniques of classical logic. To begin with, given the standard translation, every tense model $\mathcal{M} = \langle T, <, V \rangle$ can be regarded as an L_1-model, by interpreting R as $<$ and each P_i as $V(p_i)$. Then the standard translation yields the following equivalences:[9]

$\mathcal{M}, t \models \varphi$ iff $\mathcal{M} \models ST(\varphi)[x := t]$;
$\mathcal{M} \models \varphi$ iff $\mathcal{M} \models \forall x ST(\varphi)$.

The latter equivalence implies that validity of a formula of TL in a tense model is a *first-order definable property*. Validity in a temporal frame, on the other hand, turns out to be a *(universal monadic) second-order property*, as it involves universal quantification over valuations. If we treat the unary predicates from $\mathcal{P}$ as predicate variables of a second-order language L_2, every temporal frame $\mathcal{T} = \langle T, < \rangle$ can be regarded as an L_2-model, where the predicate variables represent the valuation of the atomic propositions. Let $\forall \overline{P} \varphi$ denote the universal closure of an L_2-formula φ over all predicate variables occurring in it. Then:

$\mathcal{T} \models \varphi$ iff $\mathcal{T} \models \forall \overline{P} \forall x ST(\varphi)$;
$\models \varphi$ iff $\models \forall \overline{P} \forall x ST(\varphi)$.

A TL formula φ is said to *define* the class of tense frames in which it is valid. Likewise, a sentence of FOL defines the class of tense frames in which it is true. Thus, a correspondence emerges between temporal logic and FOL as alternative languages for describing properties of time. For example, each of the formulae $\forall x \forall y \forall z(x < y \wedge y < z \rightarrow x < z)$ and (as we will soon see) $\mathsf{G}p \rightarrow \mathsf{GG}p$ defines the class of tense frames with *transitive* precedence relation. As noted in Section 3.6, not all first-order properties of temporal frames are definable by temporal formulae and, conversely, not all properties of temporal frames that are definable by formulae of TL are first-order definable. So, the correspondence is non-trivial; in fact, the theory behind it is technically quite involved. For further details on this see van Benthem (1995).

3.4 Tense Logic and McTaggart's time series

In the early twentieth century J. E. McTaggart proposed two alternative approaches to modelling time, now known as **McTaggart's time series**:

- **A-series**, characterising events as 'past', 'present', or 'future', and thus presuming a particular *present* moment, and

---

[9] Hereafter I will use the same symbol $\models$ for truth of temporal formulae and for truth of first-order sentences. Each of these will be clear from the context, so there is no risk of confusion.

- **B-series**, characterising events relatively as 'earlier' or 'later'. Here there is no concept of a 'present moment'.

Since then, there has been a debate in philosophy of time on the pros and cons of these approaches. McTaggart himself pointed out that both approaches are problematic and, consequently, argued that time itself was 'unreal'. It is not a task of logic to resolve such debates, but the main relevance of McTaggart's time-series theory here is that there is a clear affinity and close correspondence between the A-series and the modal approach on the one hand, and between the B-series and the first-order approach, on the other hand. Indeed, the first-order logic approach is grounded precisely on the B-series ontology and only evaluates the truth of formulae *globally*, in the entire model, without any reference to a 'present moment', whereas the modal-logic approach to temporal reasoning fundamentally hinges on the idea of *local truth* of formulae, relative to the present instant, which keeps shifting as time passes. Prior himself noted that correspondence Prior (1967, chapter 1). He was clearly an A-series supporter, and in the early days of temporal logic his approach was perceived as a rival to the more conventional one using first-order logic. Still, one can see how the standard translation presented in the previous section links the semantics of Prior's basic tense logic to first-order logic, thereby technically relating the A-series and B-series approaches.

3.5 Axiomatic System $\mathbf{K}_t$ for TL

Like every formal logical system, temporal logic has two major aspects: *semantic* and *deductive*. Here I present an axiomatic system for deriving validities in TL, called **the minimal tense logic $\mathbf{K}_t$**.

The list of axiom schemes of the minimal tense logic $\mathbf{K}_t$ extends that of classical propositional logic by the following four axiom schemes:

(K$_G$) $G(\varphi \rightarrow \psi) \rightarrow (G\varphi \rightarrow G\psi)$
(K$_H$) $H(\varphi \rightarrow \psi) \rightarrow (H\varphi \rightarrow H\psi)$
(GP) $\varphi \rightarrow GP\varphi$
(HF) $\varphi \rightarrow HF\varphi$

In addition to the classical rule **modus ponens (MP)**, the inference rules of $\mathbf{K}_t$ involve two **necessitation** rules for the temporal operators, as follows (where ⊢ means, as usual, 'derivable' or 'derived'):

(MP) If ⊢ φ and ⊢ $\varphi \rightarrow \psi$, then ⊢ ψ.
(NEC$_G$) If ⊢ φ, then ⊢ $G\varphi$.
(NEC$_H$) If ⊢ φ, then ⊢ $H\varphi$.

The axiomatic system $\mathbf{K}_t$ is *sound and complete* for validity in TL, that is, all TL-formulae that can be derived in $\mathbf{K}_t$ are valid in TL and vice versa.

Some general remarks are in order, applying not only to this axiomatic system, but, *mutatis mutandis*, to all others that will appear later in the Element.

1. Note that I use axiom *schemes* above. Equivalently, these can be replaced by the single axioms, like $G(p \rightarrow q) \rightarrow (Gp \rightarrow Gq)$, $p \rightarrow GPp$, and so on for any fixed atomic propositions p, q, but with the addition of the **uniform substitution** rule. That rule says that if a formula ϕ is derivable, then the result $\sigma(\phi)$ of any uniform substitution σ of formulae for the atomic propositions occurring in ϕ is derivable, too. Hereafter, I will regard the two styles of defining axiomatic systems as interchangeable.

2. The scheme (GP) can be replaced with its *dual*: (FH) $FH\varphi \rightarrow \varphi$. The latter is obtained from the former by taking the contraposition of $\varphi \rightarrow GP\varphi$, replacing $\neg\varphi$ with φ (remember that φ stands for any formula), then using the equivalences defining H and G as duals of P and F and cancelling double negations wherever they appear. It is easy to see that (GP) and (FH) are inter-derivable in that way. Semantically, they are also equivalent with respect to frame validity: the one is valid in any given tense frame iff the other one is. Likewise, the scheme (HF) can be equivalently replaced with (PG) $PG\varphi \rightarrow \varphi$.

3. The trick of replacing axiom schemes by their duals, also possibly with a *temporal shift*, can be applied likewise to any other axioms that will appear further. In particular, every TL-validity of the type $P\phi \rightarrow \psi$ can be equivalently (but, non-obviously) replaced by $\phi \rightarrow G\psi$ and vice versa. That equivalence is fairly easy to verify semantically, and is also (as expected) easily provable in $\mathbf{K}_t$: from $P\phi \rightarrow \psi$ first apply (NEC$_G$) and then (K$_G$) and (MP) to derive $GP\phi \rightarrow G\psi$; then use (GP) to derive $\phi \rightarrow G\psi$. The converse derivation from the latter formula is quite similar, using contraposition, (NEC$_H$), (K$_H$), and then again contraposition to derive $P\phi \rightarrow PG\psi$, from which $P\phi \rightarrow \psi$ is derived by using the scheme (PG). Quite analogously, $F\phi \rightarrow \psi$ and $\phi \rightarrow H\psi$ are inter-derivable.

The first two axiom schemes, (K$_G$) and (K$_H$), are the temporal correspondents of the axiom scheme (K) of the basic normal modal logic, hence the notation $\mathbf{K}_t$. The last two axiom schemes, (GP) and (HF), capture the interaction of the past and future operators. Formally, they guarantee that these operators correspond to mutually converse temporal relations, namely earlier and later, respectively.

To make the latter claim more precise, let us define a **generalised TL- frame** to be a structure $\mathcal{T} = \langle T, R_F, R_P \rangle$, where R_F and R_P are binary relations on T, and a **generalised TL-model** is such a frame endowed with a valuation in it. We can extend the semantics of TL over generalised TL-models by modifying the truth definitions of the temporal operators as follows:

- $M, t \models \mathsf{P}\varphi$ iff $M, s \models \varphi$ for some instant s, such that $t R_\mathsf{P} s$;
- $M, t \models \mathsf{F}\varphi$ iff $M, s \models \varphi$ for some instant s, such that $t R_\mathsf{F} s$.

Note that when $R_\mathsf{P} = R_\mathsf{F}^{-1}$, then the semantic clauses above correspond to the standard ones given in Section 3.2 where $\prec$ is R_F and, thus, such a generalised TL- frame can be essentially identified with the standard tense frame $\langle T, R_\mathsf{F} \rangle$. Conversely, every such standard tense frame $\mathcal{T} = \langle T, \prec \rangle$ defines a generalised TL- frame $\mathcal{T} = \langle T, \prec, \prec^{-1}, \rangle$, with respect to which the semantic clauses above correspond to the standard ones from Section 3.2.

Here are the formal claims, the routine proofs of which are left to the reader. *For every generalised* TL-*frame* $\mathcal{T} = \langle T, R_\mathsf{F}, R_\mathsf{P} \rangle$, *the following are equivalent:*

(1) $\mathcal{T} \models p \to \mathsf{GP}p.$　　　(2) $R_\mathsf{F} \subseteq (R_\mathsf{P})^{-1}.$　　　(3) $(R_\mathsf{F})^{-1} \subseteq R_\mathsf{P}.$

Analogously, the following are equivalent:

(1) $\mathcal{T} \models p \to \mathsf{HF}p.$　　　(2) $R_\mathsf{P} \subseteq (R_\mathsf{F})^{-1}.$　　　(3) $(R_\mathsf{P})^{-1} \subseteq R_\mathsf{F}.$

Putting these two claims together, we obtain that for any generalised TL-frame $\mathcal{T} = \langle T, R_\mathsf{F}, R_\mathsf{P} \rangle$, it is a standard tense frame if and only if both schemes (GP) and (HF) are valid in it. This is the precise meaning of the earlier claim that these schemes capture the interaction of the past and future operators.

There are some interesting alternative axiomatisations of TL, of which I will mention one, originally due to Wansing, see Humberstone (2016, ch. 3), which is based on capturing temporal shifts with the following axiom schemes:

Wans1: $\mathsf{G}(\mathsf{P}\varphi \to \psi) \to (\varphi \to \mathsf{G}\psi)$　　　Wans3: $\mathsf{H}(\varphi \to \mathsf{G}\psi) \to (\mathsf{P}\varphi \to \psi)$
Wans2: $\mathsf{H}(\mathsf{F}\varphi \to \psi) \to (\varphi \to \mathsf{H}\psi)$　　　Wans4: $\mathsf{G}(\varphi \to \mathsf{H}\psi) \to (\mathsf{F}\varphi \to \psi)$

As these axioms are somewhat weaker than Prior's schemes (GP) and (HF), additional inference rules are needed, as follows:

G-Nec:　　　　H-Nec:　　　　G-Mono:　　　　H-Mono:
$\dfrac{\phi}{\mathsf{G}\phi}$　　　　$\dfrac{\phi}{\mathsf{H}\phi}$　　　　$\dfrac{\phi \to \psi}{\mathsf{G}\phi \to \mathsf{G}\psi}$　　　　$\dfrac{\phi \to \psi}{\mathsf{H}\phi \to \mathsf{H}\psi}$

This system is deductively equivalent (derives the same formulae) as $\mathbf{K}_t$. In fact, Wans2 and Wans4 can be omitted, as they are derivable from the rest.

3.6 Expressing Temporal Properties in TL: Extensions of $\mathbf{K}_t$

The minimal tense logic $\mathbf{K}_t$ captures those validities of TL that do not depend on any specific assumptions concerning the properties of the temporal precedence relation. Yet, many natural properties of models of time (tense frames) can be expressed in terms of validity of temporal formulae in these frames. Taken as additional axioms, these formulae can be used to represent natural ontological assumptions about the structure of time, in the following sense. A temporal formula of TL is said to **define**, or **corresponds to**, a property $\mathcal{P}$ of tense frames if the formula is valid in all and only those frames that have the property $\mathcal{P}$. Here are some of the most important correspondences between properties of tense frames (listed in Section 2.1) and TL formulae:[10]

(REF) Any of $G\varphi \to \varphi$, $H\varphi \to \varphi$, $\varphi \to F\varphi$, or $\varphi \to P\varphi$ (reflexivity)

(TRAN) Any of $G\varphi \to GG\varphi$, $H\varphi \to HH\varphi$, $FF\varphi \to F\varphi$, or $PP\varphi \to P\varphi$
    (transitivity)

(LIN-F) $PF\varphi \to E\varphi$ (forward-linearity)

(LIN-P) $FP\varphi \to E\varphi$ (backward-linearity)

(LIN) $(PF\varphi \vee FP\varphi) \to E\varphi$ (linearity)

The following schemes assume irreflexivity of $<$.

(NOBEG) $P\top$ or $H\varphi \to P\varphi$ (time has no beginning)

(NOEND) $F\top$ or $G\varphi \to F\varphi$ (time has no end)

(DENSE) Any of $GG\varphi \to G\varphi$, $HH\varphi \to H\varphi$, $F\varphi \to FF\varphi$, or $P\varphi \to PP\varphi$
    (density)

(BEG) $H\bot \vee PH\bot$ (time has a beginning)

(END) $G\bot \vee FG\bot$ (time has an end)

The following schemes also assume (at least) transitivity of $<$.

(DISCR-F) $(F\top \wedge \varphi \wedge H\varphi) \to FH\varphi$ (forward-discreteness, assuming linearity)

(DISCR-P) $(P\top \wedge \varphi \wedge G\varphi) \to PG\varphi$ (backward-discreteness, assuming linearity)

(D-COMPL) $A(H\varphi \to FH\varphi) \to (H\varphi \to G\varphi)$ (Dedekind completeness)

(WELLORD) $H(H\varphi \to \varphi) \to H\varphi$ (transitivity plus well-ordering)

(IND$_G$) $F\varphi \wedge G(\varphi \to F\varphi) \to GF\varphi$ (forward induction)

(IND$_H$) $P\varphi \wedge H(\varphi \to P\varphi) \to HP\varphi$ (backward induction)

(FIN-INT) $IND_G \wedge IND_H$ (finite intervals)

Here is a sample of claims of correspondences from the list above, with proofs:

(TRAN) First, note that the latter two of these four schemes are obtained as duals of the former two, hence the remark in Section 3.5 applies. So, it suffices to show that each of the latter two schemes corresponds to transitivity of the precedence relation. For the last one, that follows from the claim below.

For any tense frame $\mathcal{T} = (T, <)$:

    $\mathcal{T} \models PPp \to Pp$ *if and only if $<$ is transitive.*

---

[10] Recall that $Ep = Pp \vee p \vee Fp$ and $Ap = Hp \wedge p \wedge Gp$.

Proof: Left-to-right direction: Suppose that $\mathcal{T} \models \mathsf{PP}p \to \mathsf{P}p$. Take any $s, t, u \in T$ such that $u < s$ and $s < t$. Define a model $\mathcal{M} = (\mathcal{T}, V)$ such that $V(p) = \{u\}$. Then $\mathcal{M}, s \models \mathsf{P}p$, hence $\mathcal{M}, t \models \mathsf{PP}p$. Thus, $\mathcal{M}, t \models \mathsf{P}p$ by the assumption. Then, there is $v \in T$ such that $v < t$ and $\mathcal{M}, v \models p$. Since $V(p) = \{u\}$, it follows that $v = u$, so $u < t$. Thus, $<$ is transitive.

Right-to-left direction: Suppose that $<$ is transitive. Consider any model $\mathcal{M} = (T, <, V)$ and $t \in T$. We will prove that $\mathcal{M}, t \models \mathsf{PP}p \to \mathsf{P}p$. Suppose $\mathcal{M}, t \models \mathsf{PP}p$. Then there are $s, u \in T$ such that $u < s$, $s < t$, and $\mathcal{M}, u \models p$. Then, by transitivity, $u < t$, hence $\mathcal{M}, t \models \mathsf{P}p$. Thus, $\mathcal{M}, t \models \mathsf{PP}p \to \mathsf{P}p$, for any $t \in T$ and model $\mathcal{M} = (T, <, V)$. Therefore, $\mathcal{T} \models \mathsf{PP}p \to \mathsf{P}p$.　　Q.E.D.

The claim and proof for the other transitivity schemes are quite analogous.

(LIN-F) Consider any tense frame $\mathcal{T} = (T, <)$. It suffices to prove that, for a fixed atomic proposition q:

$$\mathcal{T} \models \mathsf{PF}q \to (\mathsf{P}q \lor q \lor \mathsf{F}q) \text{ if and only if } < \text{ is forward-linear.}$$

Proof: I will prove the right-to-left direction. Suppose $<$ is forward-linear.

Consider any valuation V in $\mathcal{T}$ and let $\mathcal{M} = (\mathcal{T}, V)$. Let $t \in T$. I will show that $\mathcal{M}, t \models \mathsf{PF}q \to (\mathsf{P}q \lor q \lor \mathsf{F}q)$. Suppose $\mathcal{M}, t \models \mathsf{PF}q$. Let $s < t$ be such that $\mathcal{M}, s \models \mathsf{F}q$. Then, $\mathcal{M}, u \models q$ for some u such that $s < u$.

Since $<$ is forward-linear, either $u < t$, or $t = u$, or $t < u$.

Respectively, either $\mathcal{M}, t \models \mathsf{P}q$ or $\mathcal{M}, t \models q$, or $\mathcal{M}, t \models \mathsf{F}q$.

Thus, $\mathcal{M}, t \models \mathsf{P}q \lor q \lor \mathsf{F}q$. Therefore, $\mathcal{M}, t \models \mathsf{PF}q \to (\mathsf{P}q \lor q \lor \mathsf{F}q)$.

This holds for every valuation V and $t \in \mathcal{T}$, hence $\mathcal{T} \models \mathsf{PF}q \to (\mathsf{P}q \lor q \lor \mathsf{F}q)$.

The other direction reverses the argument above and is left to the reader.

　　　　　Q.E.D.

(IND$_\mathsf{H}$) Consider any frame $\mathcal{T} = (T, <)$ with $<$ a strict linear ordering. Then:

$\mathcal{T} \models \mathsf{P}p \land \mathsf{H}(p \to \mathsf{P}p) \to \mathsf{HP}p$ *iff $\mathcal{T}$ is backward inductive, that is, every infinite descending sequence of instants is co-initial (cf. Section 2.1).*

Proof: Left-to-right: I will prove the contrapositive claim. Suppose there is an infinite descending sequence of instants $t_1 > t_2 > \ldots$ that is not co-initial, so there is an instant s such that $s \not< t_n$ for every $n \in \mathbb{N}$. Then, $s \neq t_n$, so, by linearity, $t_n > s$, for every $n \in \mathbb{N}$.

Now, consider a model $\mathcal{M} = (\mathcal{T}, V)$ such that $V(p) = \{t_n \mid n \in \mathbb{N}\}$.

Then $\mathcal{M}, t_1 \models \mathsf{P}p \land \mathsf{H}(p \to \mathsf{P}p)$. Indeed, $\mathcal{M}, t_2 \models p$ and for every $t < t_1$, if $\mathcal{M}, t \models p$ then $t = t_n$ for some $n \in \mathbb{N}$, hence $\mathcal{M}, t_n \models \mathsf{P}p$ because $\mathcal{M}, t_{n+1} \models p$. Thus, $\mathcal{M}, t \models p \to \mathsf{P}p$ for every $t < t_1$, so $\mathcal{M}, t_1 \models \mathsf{H}(p \to \mathsf{P}p)$.

On the other hand, $\mathcal{M}, t_1 \not\models \mathsf{HP}p$ because $\mathcal{M}, s \not\models \mathsf{P}p$.

Thus, $\mathcal{M}, t_1 \not\models \mathsf{P}p \land \mathsf{H}(p \to \mathsf{P}p) \to \mathsf{HP}p$.

Right-to-left: again, we reason by contraposition.

Suppose, $\mathcal{M} = (\mathcal{T}, V)$ is such that $\mathcal{M}, t \not\models Pp \wedge H(p \rightarrow Pp) \rightarrow HPp$ for some $t \in \mathcal{T}$. Then $\mathcal{M}, t \models Pp \wedge H(p \rightarrow Pp)$ and $\mathcal{M}, t \not\models HPp$.

By the former, $\mathcal{M}, t_1 \models p$ and $\mathcal{M}, t_1 \models p \rightarrow Pp$ for some $t_1 \prec t$. Therefore, $\mathcal{M}, t_1 \models Pp$, hence $\mathcal{M}, t_2 \models p$ for some $t_2 \prec t_1$. By transitivity of $\prec$, it follows that $t_2 \prec t$, hence $\mathcal{M}, t_2 \models p \rightarrow Pp$, so $\mathcal{M}, t_2 \models Pp$. By infinitely repeating that argument (or, reasoning by induction) we construct an infinite descending sequence $t > t_1 > t_2 > \ldots$ such that $\mathcal{M}, t_n \models p$ for every $n \in \mathbb{N}$.

Now, since $\mathcal{M}, t \not\models HPp$, there is some $s \in \mathcal{T}$ such that $\mathcal{M}, s \not\models Pp$, hence $s \not\prec t_n$ for every $n \in \mathbb{N}$. Therefore, $\mathcal{T}$ is not backward inductive.   Q.E.D.

Here are some useful remarks:

- The principle (LIN) combines forward-linearity (LIN-F) and backward-linearity (LIN-P) in a single condition. The resulting formula is, however, not sufficient to guarantee the connectedness of the temporal order. In other words, it cannot rule out disjoint timelines.
- There are alternative versions of the axiom scheme (LIN-F) and (LIN-P). For example, each of the following can be adopted for backward-linearity:

  (LIN-P') $P\varphi \rightarrow HE\varphi$

  (LIN-P'') $(P\varphi \wedge PH\neg\varphi) \rightarrow P(GP\varphi \wedge H\neg\varphi)$

  (LIN-P''') $(P\varphi \wedge P\psi) \rightarrow P(\varphi \wedge P\psi) \vee P(\varphi \wedge \psi) \vee P(\psi \wedge P\varphi)$

  (LIN-P'''') $H(H\varphi \rightarrow \psi) \vee H(H\psi \rightarrow \varphi)$

  and likewise for forward-linearity. It is a useful exercise to show that each of these is both semantically and deductively equivalent to the scheme (LIN-P).
- There are also alternative axiom schemes for discreteness, like **Hamblin's axiom** $\varphi \rightarrow FH(\varphi \vee F\varphi)$ defining forward-discreteness on linear frames.
- The scheme (WELLORD) assumes irreflexivity of $\prec$. It is also known as **Gödel-Löb's formula scheme** (GL). There is a counterpart for models with reflexive precedence relations, known as **Grzegorczyk's formula scheme**, but it looks quite different: (Grz-P) $H(H(\varphi \rightarrow H\varphi) \rightarrow \varphi) \rightarrow \varphi$. The scheme (Grz-F) is defined likewise, with H replaced by G.
- (IND$_G$) implies backward-discreteness and (IND$_H$) implies forward-discreteness, but not conversely: a time flow consisting of a copy of $\langle \mathbb{N}, < \rangle$ followed by a copy of $\langle \mathbb{Z}, < \rangle$ is backward-discrete, but it does not satisfy (IND$_G$).
- As discussed in Section 2.1, neither of the properties defined by the schemes (IND)$_G$, (IND)$_H$, (D-COMPL), (WELLORD), (FIN-INT) is definable in the first-order language L_1 (with $<$ and equality).
- An alternative scheme capturing Dedekind completeness on linear frames is (D-COMPL') $(FH\varphi \wedge F\neg\varphi \wedge G(F\varphi \rightarrow \varphi)) \rightarrow F((\varphi \wedge G\neg\varphi) \vee (\neg\varphi \wedge H\varphi))$.
- On the other hand, some simple first-order definable properties of temporal frames, such as irreflexivity or anti-symmetry, are not definable in TL.

By extending the list of axioms of $\mathbf{K}_t$ with one or more of these axiom schemes, one can capture deductively the validities of various classes of natural models of time. Many such axiomatic extensions have been proved sound and complete for the corresponding classes of temporal frames. Here is a selection of the most important such results, claiming soundness and completeness of an axiomatic extension of $\mathbf{K}_t$ for a respective class of temporal frames:

$\mathbf{K4}_t = \mathbf{K}_t + \text{(TRAN)}$: for the class of all transitive frames.

$\mathbf{S4}_t = \mathbf{K}_t + \text{(REF)} + \text{(TRAN)}$: for the class of all partial orderings.

$\mathbf{L}_t = \mathbf{K}_t + \text{(TRAN)} + \text{(LIN)}$: for the class of all strict linear orderings.

$\mathbf{N}_t = \mathbf{L}_t + \text{(NOEND)} + \text{(IND}_\mathrm{G}) + \text{(WELLORD)}$: for $\langle \mathbb{N}, < \rangle$.

$\mathbf{Z}_t = \mathbf{L}_t + \text{(NOBEG)} + \text{(NOEND)} + \text{(FIN-INT)}$: for $\langle \mathbb{Z}, < \rangle$.

$\mathbf{Q}_t = \mathbf{L}_t + \text{(NOBEG)} + \text{(NOEND)} + \text{(DENSE)}$: for $\langle \mathbb{Q}, < \rangle$.

$\mathbf{R}_t = \mathbf{L}_t + \text{(NOBEG)} + \text{(NOEND)} + \text{(DENSE)} + \text{(D-COMPL)}$: for $\langle \mathbb{R}, < \rangle$.

Each of the temporal logics listed above turns out to be *decidable* (i.e., has a decidable set of validities), which is typically shown by proving that it has the *finite model property* ('Every satisfiable formula is satisfiable in a finite model') – in most cases, with respect to non-standard finite models.

Some References

For further readings on basic systems of temporal logic, temporal axioms expressing properties of time frames, correspondence with classical logic, completeness and decidability results, and so on, see Prior (1967, Ch. 1), Rescher and Urquhart (1971, Ch. VI), Segerberg (1970), Burgess (1979), Burgess (1982b), Burgess (1982a), van Benthem (1983), Burgess (1984), Burgess and Gurevich (1985), Goldblatt (1992), Gabbay et al. (1994), van Benthem (1995), Burgess (2002), Hodkinson and Reynolds (2007), Humberstone (2016, Ch. 3).

4 Temporal Logics for Linear Time

The linear models form a very natural class of instant-based models of time. Soon after Prior's invention of tense logic, several extensions of it over linear time were proposed, both with additional axiom schemes, listed in Section 3, and with additional temporal operators, such as *Nexttime* (over forward-discrete, linear models of time) and the binary operators *Since* and *Until*, presented here.

4.1 Adding the *Nexttime* Operator

Let $\mathbf{T} = \langle T, < \rangle$ be a linear temporal frame and $s, t \in T$. Then s is called an **immediate successor of** t, denoted $t \lhd s$, if $(T, <) \models t < s \wedge \neg \exists y (t < y \wedge y < s)$. Thus, we can define a new operator X (for **neXttime** or **Tomorrow**) meaning *at every immediate successor*, with formal semantics:

$$\mathcal{M}, t \models \mathsf{X}\varphi \text{ iff } \mathcal{M}, s \models \varphi \text{ for every } s \text{ such that } t \lhd s.$$

In every forward-discrete temporal frame with no last instant, every instant has an immediate successor. Assuming also linearity, it is unique. Then, the semantics simplifies to $\mathcal{M}, t \models \mathsf{X}\varphi$ iff $\mathcal{M}, s(t) \models \varphi$. Here is an illustration of the semantics of X in a forward-discrete linear and unbounded temporal frame:

The past analogue Y of X can be defined likewise.

The operator X satisfies the K-axiom

(K$_\mathsf{X}$) $\mathsf{X}(\varphi \to \psi) \to (\mathsf{X}\varphi \to \mathsf{X}\psi)$;

and the functionality axiom, saying that the immediate successor is unique:

(FUNC) $\mathsf{X}\neg\varphi \leftrightarrow \neg\mathsf{X}\varphi$.

Using X, one can give a recursive definition of G in the temporal frame $\langle \mathbb{N}, < \rangle$, based on a fixed point characterisation of G in it, as follows:

(FP$_G^r$) $G\varphi \leftrightarrow (\varphi \wedge \mathsf{X}G\varphi)$, if $<$ is assumed reflexive.
(FP$_G^{ir}$) $G\varphi \leftrightarrow \mathsf{X}(\varphi \wedge G\varphi)$, if $<$ is assumed irreflexive.

Also, the full version of the Induction Principle (IND) for the ordering of the natural numbers $\mathbb{N}$ can be formalised:

(IND^r) $\varphi \wedge G(\varphi \to \mathsf{X}\varphi) \to G\varphi$, if $<$ is assumed reflexive.
(IND^{ir}) $\mathsf{X}\varphi \wedge G(\varphi \to \mathsf{X}\varphi) \to G\varphi$, if $<$ is assumed irreflexive.

Let us prove the validity of (IND^r), that is, that $(\mathbb{N}, \leq) \models p \wedge G(p \to \mathsf{X}p) \to Gp$.

Take any model $\mathcal{M} = (\mathbb{N}, <, V)$ and $k \in \mathbb{N}$.

Suppose $\mathcal{M}, k \models p \wedge G(p \to \mathsf{X}p)$. Then $\mathcal{M}, k \models p$ and $\mathcal{M}, k \models G(p \to \mathsf{X}p)$.

We will show by induction that $\mathcal{M}, n \models p$ for any n such that $k \leq n$. The base case is given. Assume as induction hypothesis that $\mathcal{M}, n \models p$ for some $n \in \mathbb{N}$ such that $k \leq n$. From the first assumption, we have that $\mathcal{M}, n \models p \to \mathsf{X}p$, hence $\mathcal{M}, n \models \mathsf{X}p$, therefore $\mathcal{M}, n+1 \models p$, which completes the inductive step.

By the principle of mathematical induction, $\mathcal{M}, n \models p$ for every n such that $k \leq n$, hence $\mathcal{M}, k \models Gp$. Thus, $\mathcal{M}, k \models p \wedge G(p \rightarrow Xp) \rightarrow Gp$.

Some complete axiomatic systems for extensions of $\mathbf{L}_t$ in the language with G, H, and X include:

- $\mathbf{L}_t(X) = \mathbf{L}_t + K_X + (\textbf{FUNC}) + (\textbf{FP}_G)$ axiomatises the temporal logic of linear, unbounded, forward-discrete orderings.
- $\mathbf{N}_t(X) = \mathbf{N}_t + K_X + (\textbf{FUNC}) + (\textbf{FP}_G) + (\textbf{IND})$ axiomatises the temporal logic of $\langle \mathbb{N}, s, \leq \rangle$, where $s(n) = n + 1$.

4.2 Adding *Since* and *Until*

Arguably, the most important extension of Prior's basic tense logic TL was the introduction, by Hans Kamp in 1968, of the two binary temporal operators S ('*Since*') and U ('*Until*'). The intuitive meanings of these are as follows:[11]

$\varphi S\psi$ (read "φ *since* ψ") says that
$\qquad\qquad$ *φ has been true since some past time when ψ was true.*
$\varphi U\psi$ (read "φ *until* ψ") says that
$\qquad\qquad$ *φ will hold true until some future time when ψ will be true.*

For instance, the sentence '*I will keep trying until I succeed, unless I die*' can be formalised as:

try U (succeed $\vee$ die).

As another example, '*Ever since Mia left, Joe has been unhappy and has been drinking until passing out*' can be formalised using *Since* and *Until* as:

(Joe unhappy $\wedge$ (Joe drinks U Joe passes out)) S Mia leaves

The formal semantics of S and U in a temporal model $\mathcal{M} = \langle T, <, V \rangle$ is given by the following two clauses:[12]

- $\mathcal{M}, t \models \varphi S\psi$ iff $\mathcal{M}, s \models \psi$ for some s such that $s < t$
  $\qquad\qquad$ and $\mathcal{M}, u \models \varphi$ for every u such that $s < u < t$;
- $\mathcal{M}, t \models \varphi U\psi$ iff $\mathcal{M}, s \models \psi$ for some s such that $t < s$
  $\qquad\qquad$ and $\mathcal{M}, u \models \varphi$ for every u such that $t < u < s$.

---

[11] In the philosophical logic literature, often a prefix notation for U and S is used instead, where the two arguments are swapped, i.e., $U\psi\varphi$ is used for $\varphi U\psi$.

[12] These are the 'strict' versions of S and U, as originally introduced in Kamp (1968) and prevalent in philosophy. In computer science, usually reflexive versions of their semantics are used.

Prior's basic temporal operators P and F are definable in terms of S and U:

$$P\varphi := \top S\varphi \text{ and } F\varphi := \top U\varphi.$$

Consequently, G and H are definable, too. On irreflexive, forward-discrete, linear orders, U also enables a definition of the *Nexttime* operator X:

$$X\varphi := \bot U\varphi.$$

Note that this definition fails on reflexive linear orders. In fact, X is not definable with S and U on reflexive linear orders, which shows that the irreflexive versions of S and U are more expressive than their reflexive counterparts. Indeed, the latter can be defined in terms of the irreflexive ones: $\varphi S_{ref}\psi := \psi \vee (\varphi \wedge \varphi S\psi)$ and likewise for U, but generally not vice versa.

Other natural temporal operators are definable using S and U, for instance:

- *Weak Until*:

  $$\varphi U^w \psi \equiv G\varphi \vee (\varphi U\psi).$$

  Intuitively, this still expresses 'φ until ψ', but without requiring the inevitable occurrence of ψ; if ψ never occurs, then φ must remain true forever.
- *Weak Before*, defined as a dual of U on the first argument:

  $$\varphi B^w \psi \equiv \neg(\neg\varphi U\psi).$$

  Before any (if there is one) occurrence of ψ there is an occurrence of φ.
- *(Strong) Before*, defined as: a dual of U^w on the first argument:

  $$\varphi B\psi \equiv \neg(\neg\varphi U^w \psi).$$

  There will be an occurrence of ψ, and before any such occurrence there will be an occurrence of φ.
- Likewise, *weak Since* and *weak* and *strong After* can be defined using S.
- *Release*, defined as the full dual of U: $\varphi R\psi := \neg(\neg\varphi U\neg\psi)$.
  Intuitive meaning: *the truth of φ releases the requirement for the truth of ψ.*

Kamp (1968) proved the following remarkable result concerning the expressive power of temporal languages with *Since* and *Until*:

> *Every temporal operator that is definable in FOL on a class of Dedekind complete, strict linear orderings is expressible in terms of S and U on that class.*

Kamp's theorem covers both the orders of the reals and of the integers, but not the order of the rationals. Kamp (1968) has also proved that the three-variable fragment of FOL is as expressive as the full language of FOL on all linear orders.

Stavi later proposed two more operators, S' and U', which, when added to S and U, make the temporal language expressively complete on *all linear orderings*. Yet, as shown by Gabbay (see Ch. 13 in Gabbay et al. (1994)), no finite number of new operators can make the temporal language functionally complete on all *partial* orderings.

4.3 Axiomatic Systems for *Since* and *Until*

An axiomatic system for the reflexive versions of *Since* and *Until* extends classical propositional logic with the following axiom schemes and their mirror images, with U and S, as well as G and H, swapped:

(SU1) $G\varphi \rightarrow \varphi$

(SU2) $G(\varphi \rightarrow \psi) \rightarrow \varphi U\chi \rightarrow \psi U\chi$

(SU3) $G(\varphi \rightarrow \psi) \rightarrow \chi U\varphi \rightarrow \chi U\psi$

(SU4) $\varphi \wedge \chi U\psi \rightarrow \chi U(\psi \wedge \chi S\varphi)$

(SU5) $\varphi U\psi \rightarrow (\varphi \wedge \varphi U\psi)U\psi$

(SU6) $\varphi U(\varphi \wedge \varphi U\psi) \rightarrow \varphi U\psi$

(SU7) $\varphi U\psi \wedge \chi U\theta \rightarrow (\varphi \wedge \chi)U(\psi \wedge \theta) \vee (\varphi \wedge \chi)U(\psi \wedge \chi) \vee (\varphi \wedge \chi)U(\varphi \wedge \theta)$

and the inference rules MP, NEC$_G$, and NEC$_H$.

This axiomatic system is sound and complete for the class of linear temporal frames with reflexive precedence. As steps in the soundness proof, let us check the validity of the schemes (SU4) and (SU7) in any linearly ordered frame.

Proof: For the axiom scheme (SU4), suppose that $\mathcal{M}, t \models \varphi \wedge \chi U\psi$ for some model $\mathcal{M}$ and instant t. Then there is $s > t$ such that $\mathcal{M}, s \models \psi$ and $\mathcal{M}, u \models \chi$ for every u such that $t \leq u < s$. Hence, $\mathcal{M}, s \models \chi S\varphi$. Therefore, $\mathcal{M}, s \models \psi \wedge \chi S\varphi$. Thus, it follows that $\mathcal{M}, t \models \chi U(\psi \wedge \chi S\varphi)$.

As for the last scheme (SU7), its validity is easy to explain intuitively. Take any model $\mathcal{M}$ and instant u, and suppose $\mathcal{M}, u \models \varphi U\psi \wedge \chi U\theta$. Then φ will keep being true until an instant $t > u$ is reached where ψ is true. Likewise, χ will keep being true until an instant $s > u$ is reached where θ is true. By linearity, either $t = s$, or $t < s$, or $s < t$. Now:

if $t = s$ then $\mathcal{M}, t \models (\varphi \wedge \chi)U(\psi \wedge \theta)$;

if $t < s$ then $\mathcal{M}, t \models (\varphi \wedge \chi)U(\psi \wedge \chi)$; and

if $s < t$ then $\mathcal{M}, t \models (\varphi \wedge \chi)U(\varphi \wedge \theta)$.   Q.E.D.

See the bibliographic notes for some extensions of this axiomatic system.

4.4 The Linear Time Temporal Logic (LTL)

The most popular and widely used temporal logic in computer science is the **Linear Time Temporal Logic** (LTL), in which time is regarded as a linear, discrete succession of events, placed in their instants. Thus, LTL is interpreted in models over $\langle \mathbb{N}, \leq \rangle$, where the temporal precedence ordering is assumed to be reflexive, as commonly adopted in computer science. The semantics and axiomatisation of the irreflexive case is a minor modification of the reflexive case.

4.4.1 Formal Language and Expressing Properties in LTL

The standard language of LTL involves only the future operators X and U. The formulae of LTL are defined by the formal grammar

$$\varphi ::= \perp \mid p \mid \neg\varphi \mid (\varphi \wedge \varphi) \mid X\varphi \mid (\varphi U \varphi)$$

where p ranges over a set of atomic propositions. All other propositional connectives are definable as usual, and F and G can be regarded as definable in terms of U, as before: $F\varphi := \top U\varphi$ and $G\varphi := \neg F\neg\varphi$.

The logic LTL is very suitable for expressing natural properties of *infinite computations* (modelled as infinite sequences of system states) in reactive (non-terminating) systems, such as *safety, liveness*, and *fairness*, briefly explained in Section 9.5.1. Here are two typical examples:

- A natural specification for an electronic mailing system says '*Every time when a message is sent, an acknowledgement of receipt will eventually be returned, and the message will not be marked "sent" until an acknowledgement of receipt is returned*', which can be formalised in LTL as:

  G(Sent → (¬MarkedSent U AckReturned)).

- A natural specification for a fire alarm system says '*Whenever smoke is detected, the alarm is activated at the next moment and remains activated until the fire brigade arrives (if ever)*', which can be formalised in LTL as:

  G(smoke → X(alarm ∧ (alarm U^w fire brigade)))

4.4.2 Formal Semantics of LTL

The standard models for LTL are linear time models built on the time frame $(\mathbb{N}, \leq)$, hereafter simply called **(linear)** LTL-**models**. Formally, an LTL-model is just an infinite sequence $\sigma : \mathbb{N} \to \mathcal{P}(\text{PROP})$. Especially important in the theory of LTL are the so called **ultimately periodic (UP) models**, in which a finite sequence of state labels (the **loop**) repeats forever from some position on. The length of the loop is called the **period** of the UP model. For example, here are the first seven states of an ultimately periodic LTL-model where the loop is the shaded area (positions 3-6) with period 4, which thereafter repeat forever.

Given an LTL-model σ, a position $i \in \mathbb{N}$, and a formula φ, the satisfaction relation $\models$ is defined recursively as follows:

- $\sigma, i \not\models \bot$; $\sigma, i \models p$ iff $p \in \sigma(i)$, for every $p \in \mathrm{PROP}$;
- $\sigma, i \models \neg\varphi$ iff $\sigma, i \not\models \varphi$;
- $\sigma, i \models \varphi \wedge \psi$ iff $\sigma, i \models \varphi$ and $\sigma, i \models \psi$;
- $\sigma, i \models X\varphi$ iff $\sigma, i + 1 \models \varphi$;
- $\sigma, i \models \varphi U\psi$ iff there is $j \geq i$ such that $\sigma, j \models \psi$ and $\sigma, k \models \varphi$ for every k such that $i \leq k < j$.

  Note that if $j = i$, then the second requirement, for φ, becomes vacuously true.

Here is an illustration of the semantics of U:

The derived clauses for F and G are as expected:

- $\sigma, i \models F\varphi$ iff $\sigma, j \models \varphi$ for some $j \geq i$;
- $\sigma, i \models G\varphi$ iff $\sigma, j \models \varphi$ for every $j \geq i$.

When $\sigma, 0 \models \varphi$ we write $\sigma \models \varphi$ and say that φ **is true in** σ.

A formula φ of LTL is **valid**, denoted $\models \varphi$, if it is true in every linear model; φ is **satisfiable**, if its negation is not valid, that is, if φ is true in some linear model.

The semantics of LTL can be extended to define the truth of LTL formulae at a state of a Kripke model, in terms of truth on each infinite path in the model starting from that state. See details at the end of Section 6.4.2.

4.4.3 Axiomatic System for LTL and Variations

Here is a standard axiomatic system $\mathrm{Ax_{LTL}}$ for the valid formulae in LTL, with G added as a primitive operator, extending classical propositional logic with the K-axiom for G, the K-axiom and the functionality axiom for X, and axioms providing *fixed point characterisations* of the reflexive versions of G and U:

(K$_G$) $G(\varphi \rightarrow \psi) \rightarrow (G\varphi \rightarrow G\psi)$

(K$_X$) $X(\varphi \rightarrow \psi) \rightarrow (X\varphi \rightarrow X\psi)$

(FUNC) $X\neg\varphi \leftrightarrow \neg X\varphi$

(FP$_G$) $G\varphi \leftrightarrow (\varphi \wedge XG\varphi)$

(GFP$_G$) $\psi \wedge G(\psi \rightarrow (\varphi \wedge X\psi)) \rightarrow G\varphi$

(FP$_U$) $\varphi U\psi \leftrightarrow (\psi \vee (\varphi \wedge X(\varphi U\psi)))$

(LFP$_U$) $G((\psi \vee (\varphi \wedge X\theta)) \rightarrow \theta) \rightarrow (\varphi U\psi \rightarrow \theta)$

The inference rules are Modus Ponens and the necessitation rule for G.

Let us verify the validity of the scheme (FP$_G$) in any linear LTL model. It suffices to prove the validity of $Gp \leftrightarrow (p \wedge XGp)$ for some atomic proposition p. Take any LTL model σ and suppose $\sigma, 0 \models Gp$. Then, $\sigma, i \models p$ for every $i \in \mathbb{N}$. In particular, $\sigma, 0 \models p$ and $\sigma, 1 + i \models p$ for every $i \in \mathbb{N}$. Then, $\sigma, 1 \models Gp$, so $\sigma, 0 \models XGp$. Therefore, $\sigma, 0 \models (p \wedge XGp)$. Thus, $\sigma, 0 \models Gp \rightarrow (p \wedge XGp)$.

Conversely, suppose $\sigma, 0 \models (p \wedge XGp)$. Then, $\sigma, 0 \models p$ and $\sigma, 0 \models XGp$, hence $\sigma, 1 \models Gp$, so $\sigma, 1 + i \models p$ for every $i \in \mathbb{N}$. Therefore, $\sigma, i \models p$ for every $i \in \mathbb{N}$, hence $\sigma, 0 \models Gp$. Thus, $\sigma, 0 \models (p \wedge XGp) \rightarrow Gp$.

Therefore, $\sigma \models Gp \leftrightarrow (p \wedge XGp)$, for every LTL model σ. Q.E.D.

In technical terms, the scheme (FP$_G$) says that $G\varphi$ is a *fixed point* of the operator Γ_G defined by $\Gamma_G(\theta) = \varphi \wedge X\theta$, whereas (GFP$_G$) says that $G\varphi$ is (set-theoretically, in terms of extensions) a *greatest post-fixed point* of Γ_G. Likewise, the axiom (FP$_U$) says that $\varphi U\psi$ is a *fixed point* of the operator Γ_U defined by $\Gamma_U(\theta) = \psi \vee (\varphi \wedge X\theta)$, whereas (LFP$_U$) says that $\varphi U\psi$ is a *least pre-fixed point* of Γ_U. Note that the scheme (GFP$_G$) generalises the induction axiom scheme (IND): $\varphi \wedge G(\varphi \rightarrow X\varphi) \rightarrow G\varphi$. In fact, (GFP$_G$) can be replaced by the following induction rule, which is derivable in the system Ax$_{LTL}$:

If $\vdash \psi \rightarrow \varphi \wedge X\psi$, then $\vdash \psi \rightarrow G\varphi$.

Likewise, (LFP$_U$) can be replaced by the following derivable rule:

If $\vdash (\psi \vee (\varphi \wedge X\theta)) \rightarrow \theta$, then $\vdash \varphi U\psi \rightarrow \theta$.

Moreover, if Gp is defined as $\neg(\top U\neg p)$, the axioms (FP$_G$) and (GFP$_G$) become derivable from the rest.

Proving completeness of Ax$_{LTL}$ is a non-trivial task because the fixed point axioms are not canonical, so some model-theoretic constructions such as *filtration* and *bulldozing* are needed to apply to the canonical model to produce a standard linear model for LTL. See details in, for example, Goldblatt (1992).

Satisfiability and validity in LTL are decidable. In fact, every satisfiable LTL-formula ϕ is satisfiable in an ultimately periodic model with length of the prefix and a period each bounded by exponents on the length of ϕ. The decidability also follows from a more general result (Büchi's theorem) stating decidability of the monadic second-order theory of $\mathbb{N}$ with the successor function.

Some References

For further readings on temporal logics for linear time, and on LTL, see Kamp (1968), Rescher and Urquhart (1971), McArthur (1976), Pnueli (1977), in Gabbay et al. (1980), Burgess (1982b), Burgess (1982a), Burgess (1984), Sistla and Clarke (1985), Xu (1988), Zanardo (1991), Goldblatt (1992), Manna and Pnueli (1992), Venema (1993), Gabbay et al. (1994), Reynolds (1994), Reynolds (1996), Finger, Gabbay, and Reynolds (2002), Hodkinson and Reynolds (2007), Kröger and Merz (2008), Demri et al. (2016).

5 Reasoning about Non-determinism: Models and Logics for Branching Time

The idea of branching time apparently goes back at least to the thirteenth-century philosopher William of Ockham who sought to reconcile God's foreknowledge of the future with the existence of humans' free will, and hence with moral responsibility. For that, he proposed the idea of many different possible futures, of which only one will be realised (the 'actual future'), based on humans' choices and decisions. God, being omniscient and existing beyond time, already knows that actual future, but it is still open for humans. In more recent times, the idea of branching time has repeatedly appeared in the philosophical literature, including the writings of Bergson, Peirce, Łukasiewicz, and Findlay. More explicitly that idea has also appeared in the fiction literature, for example, in Jorge Borges' 1941 story "The Garden of Forking Paths" and in various sci-fi stories on time travel.

Prior had a keen interest in the questions of indeterminism and open future. In his early works, collected in Prior (1957) he, inter alia, presented some tense-logical systems intended to handle indeterminism from the perspective of intentional logic, notably including his many-valued (essentially modal) tense logic *System Q* (in Prior, 1957, ch. V), with which one could distinguish true/false from 'unstatable yesterday' statements. The idea of formally considering forward-branching time to handle indeterminism, however, was first suggested to Prior in a letter from Kripke in 1958 in response to some ideas (and correcting a mistake) in Prior (1957).

Like William of Ockham, one of Prior's major philosophical concerns was to justify the consistency of the idea of human freedom of will and action with the notion of historical necessity underlying Diodorus Cronus' Master Argument. That eventually led him to develop two systems of branching time temporal logic: *Ockhamist* and *Peircean*, which I will present in the next two sections.

5.1 Prior's Formal Reconstruction of Diodorus Cronus' Master Argument

Recall Diodorus Cronus' Master Argument from Section 1.4. Much of Prior's work on tense logic was initially motivated by the problems concerning the relationship between time and modality raised by that argument and its conceivably fatalistic conclusion. Prior's main motivation for developing formal systems of tense logic was to formalise, reconstruct, and analyse Diodorus' argument and thus to propose a solution to the problems around (in)determinism within a formal logical system.

Here are the logical principles which Prior adopted as formalising Diodorus' assumptions, where $\square$ and $\diamond$ are the modal operators formalising (historical) *necessity* and *possibility*:

(P1) $P\phi \rightarrow \square P\phi$

> This formalises the necessity of the truth about the past, stated in (D1).

(P2) $\square(\phi \rightarrow \psi) \rightarrow (\diamond\phi \rightarrow \diamond\psi)$

> This is a variation of the normal modal logic principle K, equivalent to (D2).

(P3) $\diamond\phi_0 \wedge \neg\phi_0 \wedge G\neg\phi_0$, for some particular proposition ϕ_0.

> This is a direct formalisation of (D3).

> To these principles Prior had to add the following:

(P4) $(\phi \wedge G\phi) \rightarrow PG\phi$

> This is the most questionable additional assumption by Prior. He claimed that it was an implicit assumption in Aristotle's and Diodorus' arguments. See further a technical analysis of this assumption.

(P5) $\square(\phi \rightarrow HF\phi)$

> This is necessitation of the axiom scheme (HF) of the minimal tense logic $\mathbf{K}_t$.

Here is Prior's formal inference of the Master Argument based on (P1)-(P5):

1. $\diamond\phi_0$	by (P3)
2. $\square(\phi_0 \rightarrow HF\phi_0)$	by (P5)
3. $\diamond HF\phi_0$	by (1), (2) and (P2)
4. $\neg\phi_0 \wedge G\neg\phi_0$	by (P3)
5. $PG\neg\phi_0$	by (4) and (P4)
6. $\square PG\neg\phi_0$	by (5) and (P1)
7. $\neg\diamond HF\phi_0$	by (6)
8. $\diamond HF\phi_0 \wedge \neg\diamond HF\phi_0$ – a contradiction.	by (3) and (7)

Thus, (P1)-(P5) cannot be true together, so some of them must be rejected.

Assuming reflexivity of the precedence relation, (P4) becomes trivially true and easily derivable from the reflexivity axioms, so there is no need of it. Assuming irreflexivity, however, it is easy to see that (P4) is not valid in every temporal model. Indeed, consider the model $M = (T, <, V)$, where T is the set of all natural numbers plus all rational numbers of the type $-\frac{1}{n}$ for every positive integer n, that is, $T = \mathbb{N} \cup \{-1, -\frac{1}{2}, -\frac{1}{3}, -\frac{1}{4}, \ldots\}$, with the standard linear ordering $<$ between them, and $V(p) = \mathbb{N}$.

Then, $M, 0 \models p \wedge Gp$, but $M, 0 \not\models PGp$, hence $M, 0 \not\models (p \wedge Gp) \rightarrow PGp$.

What semantic condition on temporal frames is necessary and sufficient to ensure the validity of (P4)? It turns out to be quite simple: assuming irreflexivity of the precedence order, it is that every instant has an immediate predecessor. (If the precedence order is reflexive, then every instant is its own immediate predecessor.) This condition seems natural enough not to be considered as the essential reason for the contradiction derived above, so one should look for alternative solutions, as Prior did.

5.2 Lavenham's Deterministic Argument Formalised

The fourteenth-century scholar Richard Lavenham considered an argument, quite similar in idea to the Master Argument (of which he knew), claiming that God's foreknowledge (plus some other natural assumptions) implies the determinism of the future (i.e., the non-existence of future contingents) and hence the lack of human freedom, see Øhrstrøm and Hasle (2020).

I will present here Prior's formalisation and reconstruction of a version of that argument (not explicitly involving God's foreknowledge) for which Prior used metric versions of the basic temporal operators F and P:

$F(x)\phi$: 'ϕ will be the case in x time units'
$P(x)\phi$: 'ϕ was the case x time units ago'

Here are the basic logical principles which Prior adopted as assumptions.

(PM1) $\phi \rightarrow P(x)F(x)\phi$

> Under Prior's semantics of the temporal operators, this semantically corresponds to the forward-linearity property: a model is forward-linear precisely when going x time units back in time, and then going x units forward must end up on the same history and at the same instant.

(PM2) $\square(P(x)F(x)\phi \rightarrow \phi)$

> This is a necessitation of a scheme which, likewise, corresponds in Prior's semantics to the forward-linearity property, with similar informal justification. (In the version involving God's foreknowledge this claims God's infallibility.)

(PM3) $P(x)\phi \rightarrow \Box P(x)\phi$

This formalises the necessity of the truth about the past, stated in (D1).

(PM4) $\Box(\phi \rightarrow \psi) \rightarrow (\Box\phi \rightarrow \Box\psi)$

This is the normal modal logic principle K, equivalent to (D2).

(PM5) $F(x)\phi \vee F(x)\neg\phi$

This expresses the bivalence principle for future contingents.

Here is Prior's formalisation of Lavenham 's argument based on (PM1)-(PM5):

1. $F(y)q \rightarrow P(x)F(x)F(y)q$ by (PM1)
2. $P(x)F(x)F(y)q \rightarrow \Box P(x)F(x)F(y)q$ by (PM3)
3. $F(y)q \rightarrow \Box P(x)F(x)F(y)q$ by (1) and (2)
4. $\Box(P(x)F(x)F(y)q \rightarrow F(y)q)$ by (PM2)
5. $\Box P(x)F(x)F(y)q \rightarrow \Box F(y)q$ by (4) and (PM4)
6. $F(y)q \rightarrow \Box F(y)q$ by (3) and (5)
7. $F(y)\neg q \rightarrow \Box F(y)\neg q$ likewise
8. $F(y)q \vee F(y)\neg q$ by (PM5)
9. $\Box F(y)q \vee \Box F(y)\neg q$ by (3), (4) and (7)

Thus, assuming (PM1)-(PM5), there are no future contingents.

Note that $F(0)q$ is equivalent to q, so (9) also implies $\Box q \vee \Box \neg q$.

5.3 Prior's Theory of Branching Time

Prior argued that the main fallacy of Diodorus' Master Argument was in his assumption that whatever is, or is not, or will be, or will never be, has in the past been necessarily so – thus, in effect assuming that the future is deterministic. This corresponds to the assumptions (P1)[13] and (PM3) in Prior's formalisations presented here. Prior supported Aristotle's view (later also promoted by William of Ockham) that 'while it is now beyond the power of men or gods to affect the past, there are alternative futures between which choice is possible' (Prior 1962). Another of Prior's objections was that both arguments implicitly assume, respectively with (at least) the principles (P5) and (PM1), that there is already one actual future that is about to happen, rather than a *multitude of possibilities* for the future which have not yet been realised, so when stating truth in the future one should refer to *all of them*. Prior's philosophical analysis and the quest for invalidation of the Master Argument and Lavenham's deterministic argument led him to consider two semantic systems of temporal logic of branching time, purported to capture the *logic of historical necessity*:

> the *Peircean branching time logic*, rejecting (P5), respectively (PM1), and
> the *Ockhamist branching time logic*, rejecting (P1), respectively (PM3).

---

[13] Actually, Prior accepted (P1) under the assumption that ϕ in it does not refer to the future. He also argued that if Łukasiewicz's 3-valued logic is adopted and future contingents are assigned truth value 1/2. then (P1) does not lead to determinism.

Even though Prior considered both the Peircean and the Ockhamist semantics as providing adequate solutions to the Master Argument, he apparently
favoured the Peircean view of truth in the future and the semantics based on it.

5.4 Tree-Like Models for Branching Time: Bundled Trees

Formally, a **tree-like model of time** (or, a **branching time structure**, or just
a **tree**) is a temporal frame $\mathcal{T} = \langle T, < \rangle$ where the precedence relation $<$ is
a backward-linear partial ordering on the set of instants T, such that any two
instants have a common $<$-predecessor in T. The former condition rules out
backward-branching, while the latter ensures 'historical connectedness'. Thus,
a tree $\mathcal{T} = \langle T, < \rangle$ represents the distinct alternative possibilities for the future
that are associated with any given instant and evolve into multiple histories.

Given a branching time structure $\mathcal{T} = \langle T, < \rangle$,[14] a **history** (aka **timeline**,
chronicle, or **path**), in $\mathcal{T}$ is a maximal (i.e., not extendable by adding more
instants) set of instants in T that is linearly ordered by $<$, that is, an entire path
through the tree. A history thus represents a complete possible course of events.
We denote the set of all histories in $\mathcal{T}$ by $\mathcal{H}(\mathcal{T})$, and the set of histories passing
through a given instant t in $\mathcal{T}$ by $\mathcal{H}(t)$.

Sometimes, not all histories in a branching time structure are of interest.
Some of them may even be unwanted, as they will not, or should not, be realised. In order to define the formal semantics of branching time logics presented
further, it suffices to consider rich enough families of histories, called *bundles*.

A **bundle** in a branching time struc-
ture $\mathcal{T} = \langle T, < \rangle$ is a subset $\mathcal{H}^{\mathcal{B}}$ of
$\mathcal{H}(\mathcal{T})$, such that every instant of $\mathcal{T}$
belongs to some history from $\mathcal{H}^{\mathcal{B}}$.

A **bundled tree** is a pair $(\mathcal{T}, \mathcal{H}^{\mathcal{B}})$
where $\mathcal{T} = \langle T, < \rangle$ is a branching time
structure and $\mathcal{H}^{\mathcal{B}}$ is a bundle in it.

A **complete bundled tree** is a bun-
dled tree of the type $(\mathcal{T}, \mathcal{H}(\mathcal{T}))$, that
is, with all histories in the bundle.

A simple example of an incomplete
bundle is given on the right, consisting of all paths (each labelled with ω)
branching off from A, but excluding
A.

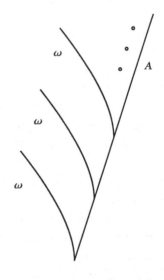

---

[14] Following the tradition in the philosophical literature, the temporal precedence relation $<$ will
be usually assumed to be irreflexive, i.e., a strict partial order, whereas in computer science, it
is usually assumed to be reflexive.

5.5 Logics for Branching Time Structures with the Basic Priorian Semantics

As we have seen, the basic Priorian temporal language TL is sufficiently expressive to capture various natural properties of branching time structures. However, its semantics does not address very well the issues with future contingencies in an indeterministic world. Indeed, the future operator F refers to *some* possible future, so $F\phi$ should be read as 'ϕ will possibly be true sometime in the future' which does not provide a coherent answer to Aristotle's question 'Will there be a sea-battle tomorrow?' in the way the two semantics for branching time mentioned earlier do. Thus, TL is not the best language to express other temporal operators or to define and axiomatise properties of branching time. Yet, note that one can still define *Always* and *Sometime* in trees, respectively as $A\varphi = H\varphi \wedge \varphi \wedge G\varphi \wedge H(H\varphi \wedge \varphi \wedge G\varphi)$ and $E\varphi = P\varphi \vee \varphi \vee F\varphi \vee P(P\varphi \vee \varphi \vee F\varphi)$.

Furthermore, axiomatising natural classes of trees in the basic Priorian semantics presents some interesting problems and I will discuss briefly here a selection of such non-trivial results.

First, a general point. Every property (respectively, class) $\mathfrak{P}$ of linear orderings, like the properties listed in Section 2.1, can be extended to a property $\mathfrak{P}^{tr}$ (respectively, class) of trees – those in which every path has the property $\mathfrak{P}$. Thus, one talks about reflexive or irreflexive trees, backward-discrete, forward-discrete (on *all* histories passing through the current instant), dense, continuous trees, and so on. In particular, we define the classes of ω-**trees**, ζ-**trees**, η-**trees**, and λ-**trees**, where every path has respectively the order type ω of the natural numbers, ζ of the integers, η of the rationals, and λ of the reals.

Now, it turns out that several natural properties of trees are definable in the language of TL, and also their respective temporal logics in the Priorian language TL are completely axiomatised by their defining axioms (which, unlike the case of first-order theories, is not something to be taken for granted). However, the axioms for most of these logics may differ essentially in the cases of irreflexive trees and of reflexive trees, so a complete axiomatisation for the latter class would not, in general, be obtained from one for the former by just adding the axiom for reflexivity.[15] I outline below a few sample results on definability and completeness for classes of irreflexive trees.

---

[15] This phenomenon is known already from linear orders, where the axiom Gödel-Löb (GL) for irreflexive well-founded trees is to be replaced by the essentially different axiom of Grzegorczyk (Grz) for reflexive well-founded trees, as noted in Section 3.6.

(AllTrees) The Priorian logic of the class all irreflexive trees TREES^{ir} is

Trees$_t$ = K_t + (TRAN) +(LIN-P)

Note that these axioms *do not define* the class TREES^{ir} within the class of all temporal frames, because they cannot force irreflexivity, nor connectedness (neither of which the language of TL can express), but they nevertheless axiomatise the validities in that class.

(DenseTrees) The Priorian logic of all dense irreflexive trees is

DenseTrees$_t$ = Trees$_t$ + (DENSE).

Thus, adding density for each path suffices for ensuring density of the whole tree, in the sense that (DENSE) *defines* the class of dense irreflexive trees within the class TREES^{ir}, and it moreover completely axiomatises its validities. The same applies, *mutatis mutandis*, for various other properties, like 'no beginning', 'no end', and so on, but *not always*. Sometimes, stronger additional axioms are needed to ensure the transfer of the property to the whole tree.

(η-Trees) Following the observations above, it turns out that the Priorian logic of the class η-TREES^{ir} of irreflexive η-trees (where each path has order type η of the rationals) is quite easy to axiomatise, by only adding the schemes for 'no beginning' and 'no end' in their simple versions ((P$\top$) and (F$\top$)):

η-Trees$_t$ = Trees$_t$ + (DENSE) + (NOBEG) + (NOEND).

(DiscreteTrees) Lastly, consider the Priorian logic **DiscreteTrees$_t$** of the class DiscrTREES^{ir} of discrete irreflexive trees. That class cannot be defined within TREES^{ir} by adding the schemes (DISCR-F) and (DISCR-F) to Trees$_t$, because (DISCR-P) is no longer valid on trees (for, going back to the immediate predecessor would widen the current set of futures, and hence the consequent PGφ may fail at some node, even though $\varphi \wedge$ Gφ may be true at that node). As for (DISCR-F), it remains valid, but it can only ensure *some* immediate successor of the current instant (on some history passing through it). So, to axiomatise the Priorian logic of all discrete irreflexive trees one apparently needs to strengthen the logic Trees$_t$ in some other ways. It turns out that it suffices to use additional non-standard inference rules of the type of the *Irreflexivity Rule* (IRR), which will be applied and explained in Section 6.3, so I will not discuss it here. Following the idea of IRR, one can add such rules to also ensure forward and backward discreteness, and thus to axiomatise the Priorian logic of all discrete irreflexive trees over Trees$_t$.

Some References

For further readings on determinism and indeterminism, Diodorus' Master Argument, logics and models for branching time, see Prior (1967), Rescher and Urquhart (1971, ch. VII), Thomason (1970), Burgess (1978), Thomason (1984), Øhrstrøm and Hasle (1995, Chapters 2.6 and 3.2), Braüner, Øhrstrøm, and Hasle (2000), Ploug and Øhrstrøm (2012), Correia and Iacona (2013), Müller (2014), Rumberg (2016), Øhrstrøm (2019), Belnap, Müller, and Placek (2022), Copeland (2022), Conradie, Marais, and Goranko (2023).

6 The Peircean Branching Time Logic PBTL

The most distinctive feature of Prior's **Peircean branching time logic**,[16] hereafter denoted by PBTL, is that there is no 'actual future' and the one that will eventually take place is yet undetermined at present and is only a mere possibility. Temporal statements and formulae of PBTL are evaluated at instants, just as in TL, but 'true in the future' now means *true in all possible futures*. Thus, the intuitive Peircean meaning of Fϕ is '*it is necessarily the case that ϕ will hold sometime in the future*'.

6.1 Language, Models, and Semantics of PBTL

Given a set of atomic propositions PROP, the set of formulae of PBTL can be recursively defined by the following formal grammar, where $p \in \mathrm{PROP}$:

$$\varphi := \bot \mid p \mid \neg\varphi \mid (\varphi \wedge \varphi) \mid \mathsf{P}\varphi \mid \mathsf{F}\varphi \mid \mathsf{G}\varphi.$$

All other propositional connectives are definable as usual and $\mathsf{H} := \neg\mathsf{P}\neg$, as in the Priorian language. However, note that in terms of the Peircean meaning of truth in the future, the two future operators F and G are both 'strong', in the sense of quantifying over *all* futures, and no longer dual to each other, so they are both taken as primitives. Their respective duals, which are now regarded as *weak* temporal operators, are defined as $\mathsf{f} := \neg\mathsf{G}\neg$ and $\mathsf{g} := \neg\mathsf{F}\neg$. Respective (strong and weak) versions of *Nexttime*, *Since* and *Until* can be added, too.

  Given a tree-like model of time $\mathcal{T} = \langle T, < \rangle$, a **Peircean valuation**, or an **instant-based valuation**, in $\mathcal{T}$ is a mapping $V : \mathrm{PROP} \to \mathcal{P}(T)$ which (just as in TL) assigns to every $p \in \mathrm{PROP}$ a set of instants $V(p) \subseteq T$ on which p is declared true. A **Peircean branching time model** (PBTL-model) is a tuple $\mathcal{M} = \langle T, <, V \rangle$, where $\langle T, < \rangle$ is a tree and V is a Peircean valuation in it. Figure 2 illustrates a PBTL-model, involving only one atomic proposition p.

---

[16] Also called 'Antactualist Indeterminist logic' in Burgess (1978) and Burgess (1980).

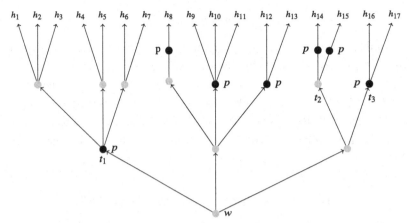

Figure 2 A Peircean branching time model, where p is true at the black nodes

The formulae of PBTL are evaluated in Peircean branching time models. The basic semantic notion is **truth of a formula of** PBTL **at an instant in a given** PBTL-**model**, defined recursively on the structure of the formulae. The semantic clauses for the truth-functional connectives and for the past operator P (and its dual H) are the same as in TL (Section 3.2), so I only present here the semantic clauses for the future operators F and G:

- $M, t \models F\varphi$ iff for all histories $h \in \mathcal{H}(t)$, there is some instant $t' \in h$ such that $t < t'$ and $M, t' \models \varphi$;
- $M, t \models G\varphi$ iff for all histories $h \in \mathcal{H}(t)$ and for all instants $t' \in h$ such that $t < t'$, it holds that $M, t' \models \varphi$.

  Since every successor t' of t lies on some history $h \in \mathcal{H}(t)$, this clause equivalently simplifies to the truth clause for G in the semantics of TL:

- $M, t \models G\phi$ iff $M, t' \models \phi$ for all t' such that $t < t'$.

The respective clauses for f and g can now be computed as follows:

- $M, t \models f\phi$ iff there is $h \in \mathcal{H}(t)$ and $t' \in h$ such that $t < t'$ and $M, t' \models \phi$.
  This clause equivalently simplifies to the one for F in the semantics of TL:
  $M, t \models f\phi$ iff there is t' such that $t < t'$ and $M, t' \models \phi$.
- $M, t \models g\phi$ iff $M, t' \models \phi$ for some $h \in \mathcal{H}(t)$ and every $t' \in h$ such that $t < t'$.

For example, in the model M on Figure 2, $M, w \models Fp$, since p is true at some future instant on *each* history starting in w.

Thus, in the Peircean semantics, the past operators and the strong future operator G essentially retain their original semantics, but the latter now reads 'it will *necessarily* always be the case that …', where necessity is understood as 'on all possible futures'. Respectively, the dual f of G is the same as the weak future operator F of TL, whereas the Peircean F and its dual g have no equivalents in TL with the standard Priorian semantics.

6.2 Some Validities and Non-validities of PBTL

A formula φ of PBTL is PBTL-**valid**, denoted $\models_{PBTL} \varphi$, if it is true at every instant in every PBTL-model; φ is PBTL-**satisfiable**, if its negation is not PBTL-valid, that is, if φ is true in some Peircean branching time model.

Assuming an irreflexive time precedence relation, the following hold.

Some PBTL-valid formulae:

- $Pp \vee P\neg p$
- $p \rightarrow GPp$
- $FHp \rightarrow p$
- $PGp \rightarrow p$

Some non-valid formulae:

- $Fp \vee F\neg p$
  (version of principle (PM5))
- $p \rightarrow HFp$
  (weaker version of principle (P5))
- $Fp \rightarrow PFp$
  (version of principle (PM1))

Each of the non-validities listed here can be falsified in the PBTL-model $\mathcal{M}'$ obtained from the model $\mathcal{M}$ on Figure 2 by making p false at t_3 and making p true at all instants on the history h_1 above t_1, as follows.

$$\mathcal{M}', w \not\models Fp \vee F\neg p, \qquad \mathcal{M}', t_1 \not\models p \rightarrow HFp, \qquad \mathcal{M}', t_2 \not\models Fp \rightarrow PFp.$$

Thus, we see that PBTL blocks both formal derivations in Section 5.1. Note also that the Peircean semantics can invalidate the principle of excluded middle $\varphi \vee \neg\varphi$ when φ refers to future contingents, as the future is not there yet.

The Peircean semantics readily generalises to bundled trees, with just one modification: the quantification over histories in the semantic clauses is restricted to the histories in the bundle. A formula of PBTL is **bundled tree valid (BT-valid)** if it is true on every branch of every Peircean bundled tree model. Burgess (1980) has proved that PBTL-validity and BT-validity coincide, and also that PBTL-validity is decidable.

6.3 Axiomatic Systems for PBTL

I will present a sound and complete axiomatic system Ax_{PBTL}^B for the PBTL-validities with strict (irreflexive) precedence relation, with no beginning and no endpoints (these constraints are mostly for technical convenience). The system Ax_{PBTL}^B is a variation of the system presented in Burgess (1980) and extends $K4_t$ (cf. Section 3.6) with axiom schemes written in terms of H, P, G, and f (corresponding to the Priorian F in TL) with the following additional schemes:

(PBTL 1) $H\varphi \rightarrow P\varphi$ (no beginning)

(PBTL 2) $G\varphi \rightarrow (F\varphi \wedge g\,\varphi)$ (no end)

(PBTL 3) $FG\varphi \rightarrow GF\varphi$ (eventually always implies cofinally)

(PBTL 4) $FF\varphi \rightarrow F\varphi$ (transitivity)

(PBTL 5) $(H\varphi \wedge \varphi \wedge G\varphi) \rightarrow GH\varphi$ (linearity of the past)

(PBTL 6) $(H\varphi \wedge \varphi \wedge g\,\varphi) \rightarrow g\,H\varphi$ (linearity of the past on a history)

Checking the validity of these schemes is a relatively routine task.

The inference rules of $\mathrm{Ax}^B_{\mathrm{PBTL}}$ involve, besides the standard rules Modus Ponens, G-Necessitation, and H-Necessitation, also the following special **Irreflexivity Rule:**[17]

(IRR) : $\dfrac{(p \wedge H\neg p) \rightarrow \varphi}{\varphi}$, assuming that p does not occur in φ.

The deductive use of this kind of non-standard rule is not yet well understood (it is not even known when such rules can be omitted without loss of deductive power), but here IRR is used in the proof of completeness to force irreflexivity of the temporal precedence relation $<$, which is not definable by an axiom of PBTL. The semantic argument to justify that IRR preserves validity in tree-like PBTL-models with an irreflexive precedence relation (i.e., that it is safe to add it to the axiomatic system as an inference rule) is simple: if the conclusion φ can be falsified at some instant t in some irreflexive PBTL-model $\mathcal{M}$, then the valuation of p in $\mathcal{M}$ can be altered to make p true only strictly in the future of t, and that will not affect the falsity of φ at t, as p does not occur in φ. However, the resulting valuation falsifies the premise of IRR at t because the antecedent $\neg p \wedge H\neg p$ is true there. By contraposition, if the premise cannot be falsified (hence, is valid) then the conclusion cannot be falsified, either.

Zanardo (1990) provided another sound and complete axiomatisation of the PBTL validities, which is a variation of $\mathrm{Ax}^B_{\mathrm{PBTL}}$ where the rule IRR is replaced by an infinite family of rather elaborate additional axiom schemes.

---

[17] A historical note is in order here. This rule is a simplified version of the rule R3 in Burgess (1980), but its use and importance were not discussed there. A more general and elaborated version of this rule, for multimodal languages, was independently presented in Gabbay (1981). It was discussed, promoted, and used there to completely axiomatise some classes of irreflexive frames, whence it became widely known as Gabbay's Irreflexivity Rule. Several variations and generalisations of this rule have been studied and applied since then. More references to such rules appear further in the Element.

6.4 Computation Tree Logic CTL

Branching time logics are extensively used in computer science. The most popular one is the **computation tree logic** CTL. It is a special case of a simple language extension of PBTL. The logic was introduced as a temporal logic for formal specification and verification of properties of infinite computations in transition systems, where the computations are modelled by infinite sequences of states in the transition system, generated by following the transition relation in it. The logic CTL became widely used due to the computational efficiency of *model checking* (checking truth of formulae in models) in it.

6.4.1 The Language and Semantics of CTL

The standard language of CTL involves combined operators pairing temporal operators X, G, U with immediately preceding quantifiers over paths (histories). Thus, the non-propositional connectives of CTL are[18] $\forall X\varphi$, $\exists X\varphi$, $\forall G\varphi$, $\exists G\varphi$, $\forall(\varphi U\psi)$, and $\exists(\varphi U\psi)$, The operators $\forall G\varphi$ and $\exists G\varphi$ are notational variants of the Peircean temporal operators G and g, whereas F and f are definable respectively as $F\psi := \forall(\top U\psi)$ and $f\psi := \exists(\top U\psi)$. In fact, $\forall X\varphi$, $\forall(\varphi U\psi)$, and $\exists(\varphi U\psi)$ suffice as primitives, as the others listed here are definable from them. Thus, the language of CTL is essentially an extension of PBTL with weak and strong versions of X and U.

Here is a generic example of a property of the computations in a transition system where several processes interact:

'*If the process σ is eventually enabled on some computation starting from the current state, then on every computation starting from that state, whenever σ is enabled it will remain enabled on some computation starting then, until the process τ is disabled.*'

This property can be formalised in CTL as

$$\exists F \, enabled_\sigma \rightarrow \forall G(enabled_\sigma \rightarrow \exists(enabled_\sigma \, U \, disabled_\tau)).$$

The logic CTL is interpreted on so-called **computation trees**, which are PBTL-models where every history has the order type of the natural numbers, usually denoted by ω. Such trees are also called ω-**trees**. The semantics of CTL on ω-trees extends in a straightforward way the semantics of PBTL with clauses for the weak and strong versions of X and U, by respective quantification over histories combined with the LTL semantics for X and U. More precisely, consider any ω-tree $\mathcal{T} = \langle T, < \rangle$. Then any history h on it can be

---

[18] The more common notation in the computer science literature uses quantifiers instead of the modalities of historical necessity □ and possibility ◇ for quantification over paths in CTL.

explicitly given as an infinite sequence of nodes in the tree, representing consecutive instants: $h(0), h(1), h(2), \ldots$. Besides, for every instant t in $\mathcal{T}$, $t = h(n)$ for some history h and $n \in \mathbb{N}$. Furthermore, $t = h'(n)$ for *every* other such history h' that passes through t. Now, here are the semantic clauses for the truth of the strong versions of X and U at the node $t = h(n)$ of the ω-tree $\mathcal{T}$:

- $M, h(n) \models \forall X\varphi$ iff *for all histories* $h' \in \mathcal{H}(h(n))$, $M, h'(n + 1) \models \varphi$;
- $M, h(n) \models \forall(\varphi U\psi)$ iff *for all* $h' \in \mathcal{H}(h(n))$ *there is* $j \in \mathbb{N}$ *such that* $M, h'(n + j) \models \psi$ *and* $M, h'(n + i) \models \varphi$ *for every* $i \in \mathbb{N}$ *such that* $0 \le i < j$.

The semantic clauses of $EX\varphi$ and $\exists(\varphi U\psi)$ are defined likewise, with existential instead of universal quantification over histories. I leave it to the reader to see that the respective semantic clauses for $\forall G\varphi$ and $\exists G\varphi$ are equivalent to those in the Peircean semantics of G and g in Section 6.1.

Satisfiability and validity in CTL are defined, as expected, by restriction of the notions of satisfiability and validity in PBTL to models on ω-trees. The semantics of CTL extends to bundled trees just as the semantics of PBTL does.

6.4.2 Unfoldings and Semantics of CTL on Kripke Models

Computation trees are naturally generated as *unfoldings* of discrete transition systems and represent the possible infinite computations arising in such systems. Intuitively, a transition system is simply a **Kripke model**, that is, a structure of the type $M = \langle W, R, L \rangle$, where W is a non-empty set of states, $R \subseteq W^2$ is a binary **transition relation** (aka **accessibility relation**) on states, and $L : W \to \mathcal{P}(\text{PROP})$ is a **labelling function** (aka **state description**), which assigns to every state $s \in W$ the set $L(s)$ of atomic propositions that are true at s, called the **label** (or **description**) of that state. For any states $s, t \in W$; if $(s, t) \in R$ we say that t **is an R-successor of** s, and also write sRt or Rst.

Given a Kripke model $M = \langle W, R, L \rangle$ and a state $s \in W$, the **unfolding of** M **from the state** s is a (generally infinite) tree-like model $\widehat{M}$ rooted at a copy $\hat{s}$ of s, constructed by the following intuitively described procedure. First, starting with the copy $\hat{s}$ of s, with the same label as s, produce a *new copy* (not yet produced) of each R-successor of s, with the same label as the original, and make these copies successors of $\hat{s}$ with respect to the transition relation in the unfolding. Then, apply the same procedure to each newly produced copy of a state, and then do the same with these, and so on. Put more explicitly, the unfolding produces a copy of the starting state, then grafts onto it a (new) copy of each of its successors, then grafts onto each of them (again, new) copies of its successors, and so on. Or, put recursively, the unfolding produces a copy of the root (starting) state, then grafts onto it a (new) copy of each of its successors,

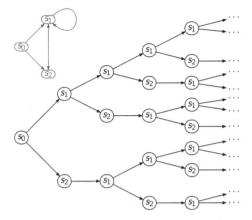

Figure 3 An unfolding of a Kripke model (on the top left) from a state (s_0)

and then onto each of these successors, taken as a root, grafts a copy of the unfolding from that successor.

Thus, the unfolding of a Kripke model M from the state s is a generally infinite procedure of step-by-step 'unfolding' of all paths in M starting from s into explicit histories in the resulting tree-like model. Figure 3 illustrates the unfolding of the Kripke model in the top left corner from the state s_0.

Note that every history in $\widehat{M}$ is either finite or has the order type ω, and that every R-path starting from the state s in the original Kripke model M is represented by some history in the unfolding starting from the copy of s. Conversely, every such history is a copy of a path in the original Kripke model M starting from s. Consequently, there is a one-to-one correspondence between the paths in M starting at the state s and the histories in the unfolding of M starting from s. With this observation in mind, using the unfolding construction one can extend in a straightforward way the semantics of CTL from ω-trees to arbitrary Kripke models. To ensure that the results of the unfoldings are always ω-trees and to avoid the technical inconvenience of dealing with states with no successors, the semantics of CTL is usually restricted to *serial* Kripke models, where every state has at least one successor. This can always be achieved by making the states with no successors 'idling', that is, having themselves as their only successors.

6.4.3 Extension of the Semantics of LTL to Kripke Models

The semantics of LTL in linear models can be extended to models based on ω-trees as follows. With every such model M and a state s in it, we associate the set of all linear LTL-models based on the paths starting from s in M, denoted as $\text{Paths}(M, s)$. Now, LTL formulae can be evaluated in pairs (M, s) as follows.

$$(M, s) \models \varphi \text{ iff } \sigma \models \varphi \text{ for all paths } \sigma \in \text{Paths}(M, s).$$

Then we say that φ **is universally true in** $(\mathcal{M}, s)$, denoted $\mathcal{M}, s \models_\forall \varphi$.

Likewise, we define **existential truth of** φ **in** $(\mathcal{M}, s)$, denoted $\mathcal{M}, s \models_\exists \varphi$, if $\sigma \models \varphi$ *for some path* $\sigma \in \text{Paths}(\mathcal{M}, s)$.

Now, using the unfolding construction one can further extend, in a straightforward way, these definitions to truth of LTL formulae at states of arbitrary Kripke models. As it turns out, in order to check the universal or existential truth of an LTL formula at a state in a finite Kripke model, it suffices to check its truth only on all *ultimately periodic paths* (cf. Section 4.4.2) in the model starting from that state. Furthermore, it suffices to consider only those (finitely many!) such paths where the lengths of the prefix and the period are bounded above by the value of some exponential function on the length of the formula; see further details in, for example, Demri et al. (2016, ch. 6).

6.4.4 A Sound and Complete Axiomatic System for CTL

To obtain a sound and complete axiomatisation of CTL for the class of all ω-trees (equivalently, for the class of all serial Kripke models) it suffices to replace the axioms of LTL with their path-quantified versions, as follows.

Axiom schemes:

(CL) Enough classical tautologies.

(K$_X$) $\forall X(\varphi \to \psi) \to (\forall X\varphi \to \forall X\psi)$

(D$_X$) $\exists X\top$

(FP$_{\exists G}$) $\exists G\varphi \leftrightarrow (\varphi \wedge \exists X \exists G\varphi)$;

(FP$_{\forall G}$) $\forall G\varphi \leftrightarrow (\varphi \wedge \forall X \forall G\varphi)$;

(FP$_{\exists U}$) $\exists(\varphi U\psi) \leftrightarrow (\psi \vee (\varphi \wedge \exists X \exists(\varphi U\psi)))$;

(FP$_{\forall U}$) $\forall(\varphi U\psi) \leftrightarrow (\psi \vee (\varphi \wedge \forall X \forall(\varphi U\psi)))$.

The inference rules are Modus Ponens and the $\forall G$-Necessitation rule: if $\vdash \varphi$, then $\vdash \forall G\varphi$.

The logic CTL has the *finite model property*: every satisfiable CTL-formula is satisfiable in a finite Kripke model. Consequently, satisfiability and validity in CTL are decidable (more precisely, EXPTIME-complete).

Some References

For further readings on the Peircean branching time logic PBTL, on CTL, and on other variations of PBTL, see Burgess (1978), Burgess (1979), Burgess (1980), Emerson and Clarke (1982), Ben-Ari, Pnueli, and Manna (1983), Emerson and Sistla (1984), Emerson and Halpern (1985), Gurevich and Shelah (1985), Emerson (1990), Zanardo (1990), Goldblatt (1992), Stirling (1992), Gabbay et al. (1994), Baier and Katoen (2008), Demri et al. (2016).

7 The Ockhamist Branching Time Logic OBTL

The other system of temporal logic for branching time proposed by Prior was based on the idea, going back to William of Ockham, that while the past is fixed and cannot be changed, there are many possible futures and one of them is the *actual future*. We, the humans, may not know it, and may not have the power and free will to act so as to change the currently expected course of events, but God (being beyond time) already knows that actual future. This idea purports to explain God's omniscience, including knowledge of the actual future, with humans' ability to apply free will and alter the course of events, thus accounting for the world's non-determinism. The defining feature of the resulting system branching time logic, now called **Ockhamist branching time logic**, hereafter abbreviated as OBTL, is that it evaluates the truth of formulae on tree-like models, just like in the Peircean semantics, but now *with respect to both a current instant and a history passing through that instant*, representing the currently assumed *actual history*. Thus, the intuitive Ockhamist meaning of $F\phi$ is 'ϕ *will be true sometime in the future on the actual history*'. This idea will be made precise here.

7.1 Language and Models for OBTL

The language of OBTL contains Prior's standard temporal operators F and P, as well as the modal operator $\diamond$ intuitively interpreted as **historical possibility**.[19] Their respective duals, G, H, and $\square$ (**historical necessity**) can then be taken as definable.[20] Technically, $\diamond$ and $\square$ are interpreted as (existential and universal) quantifiers over histories. Given a set of atomic propositions PROP, the set of formulae of OBTL can be recursively defined by the following formal grammar:

$$\varphi := p \in \text{PROP} \mid \bot \mid \neg\varphi \mid (\varphi \wedge \varphi) \mid P\varphi \mid F\varphi \mid \diamond\varphi.$$

All other propositional connectives are assumed definable as usual. Optionally, *Nexttime*, *Since* and *Until* can be added, too.

As in the Peircean semantics, in the **Ockhamist semantics** formulae are interpreted in branching time structures $\mathcal{T} = \langle T, < \rangle$. The notion of a history (path), the set $\mathcal{H}(\mathcal{T})$ of all histories in $\mathcal{T}$, and the set $\mathcal{H}(t)$ of histories in $\mathcal{T}$ passing through a given instant t are defined as in Section 5.4.

The formal context of evaluation of formulae in the Ockhamist semantics is a history/instant pair (h, t), where $h \in \mathcal{H}(\mathcal{T})$ and $t \in h$. Such a pair will be conceived to represent the set of all instants $\{s \in h \mid t \leq s\}$, and will be called a **branch (on the history h starting at the instant t)**. Intuitively,

---

[19] This is different from the Diodorean notion of possibility as truth now or in some future instant.

[20] This is an almost arbitrary choice, made only for historical reasons, following Prior. Instead, the strong operators G and H, and $\square$ can be taken as primitives and the weak ones as definable.

the branch (h, t) also represents an instant t together with an 'actual' history passing through it.[21] The set of all branches in $\mathcal{T}$ will be denoted by $\mathcal{B}(\mathcal{T})$.

An **Ockhamist valuation** in $\mathcal{T} = \langle T, \prec \rangle$ is a mapping $V: \mathrm{AP} \to \mathcal{P}(\mathcal{B}(\mathcal{T}))$ assigning to every $p \in \mathrm{AP}$ the set of branches $V(p) \subseteq \mathcal{B}(\mathcal{T})$ on which p is true. An **Ockhamist branching time model** (OBTL-model) is a tuple $\mathcal{M} = \langle T, \prec, V \rangle$ where $\langle T, \prec \rangle$ is a tree and V is an Ockhamist valuation in it.

The question of why the truth of atomic propositions is evaluated relative to history/instant pairs, rather than on instants alone, arises naturally. Indeed, Prior himself was undecided on that question and he even wrote that "atomic propositions should not contain traces of futurity,"[22] but eventually he considered both options, and also the idea of a two-sorted language with two different kinds of atomic propositions, *instant-based* and *history/instant-based*. There are, however, good technical reasons to prefer the more general approach to Ockhamist valuations adopted here:

1. Atomic propositions in a formal propositional logical language are often also treated in the formal logic literature as *propositional variables*, that is, variables ranging over propositions. Technically, both play similar roles, even though they are conceptually different objects. In OBTL such a propositional variable can be assigned any proposition as a value that involves futurity, hence its truth is generally dependent on the entire branch.
2. Instant-based atomic propositions are a special case of branch-based ones, as every standard, instant-based, valuation V can be transformed into an *equivalent* (in a precise sense) Ockhamist valuation V^O defined by $V^O(p) = \{(h, t) \in \mathcal{B}(\mathcal{T}) \mid t \in V(p)\}$. This idea is formally applied in Section 7.4.
3. Moreover, an instant-based atomic proposition can be technically simulated by prefixing a branch-based one with $\square$. Indeed, as we will see in the formal semantics, the truth of the formula $\square p$ only depends on the instant t in the branch (h, t) where the formula is evaluated, thus essentially representing an instant-based atom. Thus, the more general approach is formally superior. See also a discussion on this issue in Brown (2014).

7.2 Expressing Temporal Statements in OBTL

Here are some examples of expressing temporalised statements in OBTL, so far referring to its intuitive semantics:

---

[21] Note that t uniquely determines the past (before t) on that history, so it is only the future branch of that history that the pair (h, t) has to additionally specify, hence the name 'branch'.

[22] Sometimes, however, the 'trace of futurity' is subtle, as in 'I am going to complete this book'.

- '*Life on Earth will eventually cease to exist*'

  FG¬LifeOnEarth

- '*Necesssarily, life on Earth will eventually cease to exist*'

  □FG¬LifeOnEarth

- '*Life on Earth may eventually cease to exist*'

  ◇FG¬LifeOnEarth

- '*If a new global war breaks out in the future, life on Earth will eventually necessarily cease to exist, but humanity can change the course of history to avoid a new global war*'

  (F War → F□G¬LifeOnEarth) ∧ ◇¬F War

- '*On every possible future history where life on Earth will eventually cease to exist, every day when there is life on Earth humanity can change the course of history so that there will be life on Earth the day after.*'

  □(FG¬LifeOnEarth → G(LifeOnEarth → ◇X LifeOnEarth))

(Here X is the *Nexttime* operator, as in LTL.)

7.3 Formal Semantics of OBTL

Now, I will present the formal Ockhamist semantics of OBTL formulae.

7.3.1 Ockhamist Truth on a Branch in an OBTL Model

Truth of an OBTL-**formula in an** OBTL-**model** $\mathcal{M} = \langle T, \prec, V \rangle$ **on /relative to a branch** (h, t), with $h \in \mathcal{H}(\mathcal{M})$ and $t \in h$, is defined recursively as follows:

- $\mathcal{M}, (h, t) \models p$ iff $(h, t) \in V(p)$, for any $p \in \text{AP}$
- $\mathcal{M}, (h, t) \not\models \bot$; $\mathcal{M}, (h, t) \models \neg\varphi$ iff $\mathcal{M}, (h, t) \not\models \varphi$
- $\mathcal{M}, (h, t) \models \phi \wedge \psi$ iff $\mathcal{M}, (h, t) \models \phi$ and $\mathcal{M}, (h, t) \models \psi$
- $\mathcal{M}, (h, t) \models \mathsf{F}\phi$ iff $\mathcal{M}, (h, t') \models \phi$ for some instant $t' \in h$ such that $t \prec t'$
- $\mathcal{M}, (h, t) \models \mathsf{P}\phi$ iff $\mathcal{M}, (h, t') \models \phi$ for some instant $t' \in h$ such that $t' \prec t$
  (The requirement $t' \in h$ is redundant here, due to backward linearity.)
- $\mathcal{M}, (h, t) \models \Diamond\phi$ iff $\mathcal{M}, (h', t) \models \phi$ for some history $h' \in \mathcal{H}(t)$.

The truth clauses for the definable connectives are as expected. In particular:

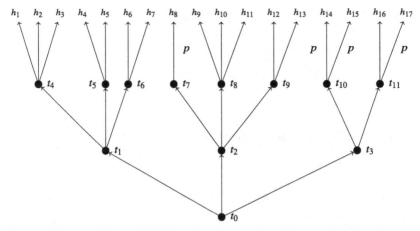

Figure 4 An Ockhamist branching time model

- $M, (h, t) \models G\phi$ iff $M, (h, t') \models \phi$ for every instant $t' \in h$ such that $t \prec t'$
- $M, (h, t) \models H\phi$ iff $M, (h, t') \models \phi$ for every instant $t' \in h$ such that $t' \prec t$
- $M, (h, t) \models \Box\phi$ iff $M, (h', t) \models \phi$ for every history $h' \in \mathcal{H}(t)$.

For example, consider the OBTL-model M in Figure 4, where p is true in the following branches, also indicated in the figure: $(h_8, t_7), (h_{14}, t_{10}), (h_{15}, t_{10}),$ (h_{17}, t_{11}). Then, the following hold:

- $M, (h, t_0) \models \neg p$ for any history $h \in \mathcal{H}(t_0)$.
- Therefore, $M, (h, t_0) \models \Box\neg p$ for any history $h \in \mathcal{H}(t_0)$.
- $M, (h_{14}, t_{10}) \models \Box p$.
- $M, (h_{16}, t_{11}) \models \neg p \wedge \Diamond p \wedge \neg\Box p$
- $M, (h_{17}, t_{11}) \models p \wedge \Diamond p \wedge \neg\Box p$.
- $M, (h_{14}, t_3) \models Fp \wedge F\Box p \wedge \Diamond F\neg\Box p$.
- $M, (h_{16}, t_3) \models G\neg p \wedge F\Diamond p \wedge \Diamond Fp$.
- $M, (h_8, t_2) \models F\Box p \wedge \Diamond G\neg p$.

Thus, the temporal operators in the Ockhamist semantics are essentially interpreted as they are in the linear time logics: the instant of evaluation is simply shifted backwards and forwards on the current history. Respectively, the modal operators $\Diamond$ and $\Box$ fix the current instant and quantify over the set of histories passing through it, thus $\Diamond F\varphi$ saying that 'φ holds eventually in *some* possible future', while $\Box F\varphi$ says that 'φ holds eventually in *all* possible futures', that is, φ will necessarily eventually be the case.

A formula of OBTL is **Ockhamist valid** iff it is true on every branch of every OBTL-model. Respectively, it is **Ockhamist satisfiable** iff its negation is not Ockhamist valid, that is, if it is true on some branch of some OBTL-model.

7.3.2 Some Validities and Non-validities of OBTL

First, note that every temporal formula in the language of TL that is valid in all linear-time models is also Ockhamist valid. Furthermore, Ockhamist validity is closed under □-Necessitation, G-Necessitation, and H-Necessitation, as well as under uniform substitution of formulae for (branch-based) atoms.

Here are some concrete examples of Ockhamist valid formulae:

- Unlike in the Peircean semantics, the principle of future-excluded middle $Fp \vee F\neg p$ is true on every branch at any instant which is not an endpoint (that is, has some future instant), so $F\top \to (Fp \vee F\neg p)$ is OBTL valid.
- $Pp \to \square P\diamond p$.
  Here is an informal argument for this validity. Suppose Pp is true on some current branch (h,t) in an OBTL-model. Then p is true on some branch (h,s) on the same history starting at some earlier instant s. The instant s belongs to any other history h' passing through the current instant t, and $\diamond p$ is true on (h',s), hence $P\diamond p$ is true on (h',t). Thus, $\square P\diamond p$ is true on (h,t).
- $\square Gp \to G\square p$.
  Again informally, every branch that can be reached from a current branch (h,t) in a OBTL-model by first moving to the future along h and then switching to an alternative history h', can also be reached by first switching to the alternative history h' and then moving to the future on that history. However, this argument cannot be reversed, as $G\square p \to \square Gp$ is not OBTL valid.
- $\square G\diamond Fp \to \diamond GFp$, where p is an instant-based proposition.
  (Alternatively, consider $\square G\diamond F\square p \to \diamond GF\square p$, for any p.)
  Here is a more formal argument for the special case of Ockhamist models on ω-trees. Take any OBTL-model $\mathcal{M} = \langle T, \prec, V\rangle$, where $\langle T, \prec\rangle$ is an ω-tree. Consider any branch (h,t) and suppose $\mathcal{M},(h,t) \models \square G\diamond Fp$. Take any future instant t' on h. (If there is no such instant, then GFp is vacuously true on (h,t), hence $\diamond GFp$ is also true on (h,t).) Then $\mathcal{M},(h,t') \models \diamond Fp$, hence there is a branch (h_1,t_1) such that $h_1 \in \mathcal{H}(t')$, $t' \prec t_1$, hence $t \prec t_1$, and $\mathcal{M},(h_1,t_1) \models p$. Since $h_1 \in \mathcal{H}(t)$ and $t \prec t_1$, we also have that $\mathcal{M},(h_1,t_1) \models \diamond Fp$, so we can find a new branch (h_2,t_2) such that $h_2 \in \mathcal{H}(t_1)$, $t_1 \prec t_2$, and $\mathcal{M},(h_2,t_2) \models p$. Repeating the argument above, we obtain that $\mathcal{M},(h_2,t_2) \models \diamond Fp$, so the same argument applies to (h_2,t_2), and so on. Thus, eventually an infinite sequence of branches $(h,t) = (h_0,t_0),(h_1,t_1),(h_2,t_2)\ldots$, where $t_0 \prec t_1 \prec t_2 \prec \ldots$, can be constructed so that $\mathcal{M},(h_n,t_n) \models p$ for each $n \geq 0$. This sequence generates a history h^* passing through t and each t_n. Thus, we have that $\mathcal{M},(h^*,t) \models GFp$, because p is instant-based, so equally true on (h_n,t_n) and (h^*,t_n) for each n. Therefore, $\mathcal{M},(h,t) \models \diamond GFp$. Thus, $\mathcal{M},(h,t) \models \square G\diamond Fp \to \diamond GFp$.

Note, that this proof uses a weaker form of the Axiom of Choice. For the general case (where the model is not based on an ω-tree), a transfinite induction, or the full Axiom of Choice, or an application of another equivalent non-constructive principle, like Zorn's lemma, would be needed.

- If we add the *Nexttime* operator X, then $p \wedge \Box G(p \rightarrow \Diamond Xp) \rightarrow \Diamond Gp$ is a semantically similar example of a formula valid on the class of Ockhamist tree models with reflexive precedence relation and where every instant has an immediate successor on every history passing through it.

Now, here are some Ockhamist non-valid formulae:

- The principle of the necessity of the past (P1) $P\varphi \rightarrow \Box P\varphi$ is not Ockhamist valid, and it thereby blocks Diodorus' Master Argument. It can be easily falsified in the Ockhamist model $\mathcal{M}$ on Figure 4. For example, if we add the branch (h_{17}, t_3) to the valuation of p then $\mathcal{M}, (h_{17}, t_{11}) \not\models Pp \rightarrow \Box Pp$.
- The metric principle (PM3) $P(x)\varphi \rightarrow \Box P(x)\varphi$ in Lavenham's argument is not valid, either. It can be likewise falsified in a variation of the model $\mathcal{M}$.
- However, $Pp \rightarrow \Box Pp$ is valid if p is an instant-based proposition.
- Likewise, $p \rightarrow \Box p$ is valid for any instant-based atomic proposition p, but $\phi \rightarrow \Box\phi$ is not valid for every formula ϕ.
- Each of $Fq \rightarrow \Box Fq$, $F\Box q \rightarrow \Box Fq$, and $G\Box q \rightarrow \Box Gq$.
  These can be likewise easily falsified in the Ockhamist model $\mathcal{M}$ on Figure 4.
- The principle (P4) $(\phi \wedge G\phi) \rightarrow PG\phi$ is not Ockhamist valid, either, since it is not valid on every linear model, as shown in Section 5.1.

7.3.3 Ockhamist Validity versus Bundled Trees Validity

The Ockhamist semantics generalises to bundled trees with only two small modifications:

- An Ockhamist valuation in a bundled tree $(\mathcal{T}, \mathcal{H}^{\mathcal{B}})$ assigns to any atomic proposition only branches with histories from the bundle.
- The quantification over histories in the semantic clauses for $\Diamond$ and $\Box$ is restricted to the histories in the bundle.

A formula of OBTL is **Ockhamist bundled tree valid (Ockhamist BT-valid)** if it is true on every branch of every Ockhamist bundled tree model.

Unlike in PBTL with the Peircean semantics, the generalised Ockhamist semantics on bundled trees differs in terms of validities from the standard one. Indeed, Ockhamist BT-validity is *strictly weaker* than the standard Ockhamist validity, that is, the BT-validity restricted to complete bundled trees. For example, the following formula, where p is an instant-based proposition

$$\Box G \Diamond F p \to \Diamond G F p$$

is Ockhamist valid but not Ockhamist BT-valid. The reason is that the antecedent of this formula intuitively allows one to construct an *emerging history* (or, a *limit history*) from an infinite bundle of different histories, in which p holds infinitely often. Such limit histories may not belong to the bundle in a bundled tree. Indeed, there is a falsifying Ockhamist model, built on the infinite binary tree, that is, one where every node has two successor nodes: left and right successor. Define p to be true at only those nodes which are the right successor of their parent nodes. Then consider the bundle consisting of only those paths that eventually only go left, that is, from some node onwards only left successors are selected. (Note that this is a bundle!) The antecedent $\Box G \Diamond F p$ is true at the root of that bundled tree, while the consequent $\Diamond G F p$ fails there, because there is no path in the bundle with infinitely many right successors.

Can a formula like the one just described *define* the class of all complete bundled trees within the class of all bundled trees? No, it cannot, as was proved in Zanardo, Barcellan, and Reynolds (1999).

The Ockhamist validity can be proved decidable by using Rabin's theorem of decidability of the monadic second order logic (MSO) on infinite binary trees with additional unary predicates. Rabin's theorem has also been used for several other highly non-trivial decidability results in modal and temporal logics, see Gabbay (1973), Gabbay (1975).

7.4 Embedding PBTL into OBTL

The Peircean branching time logic PBTL can be regarded as the fragment of the Ockhamist logic OBTL only involving formulae that are built from instant-based atoms by using propositional connectives, the combined future operators $\Box F$ and $\Box G$, and their duals $\Diamond G$ and $\Diamond F$, as follows. First, for every PBTL-model $\mathcal{M} = \langle T, <, V \rangle$ we define the Ockhamist model $\mathcal{M}^O$ obtained from $\mathcal{M}$ by replacing the Peircean valuation V with the Ockhamist valuation V^O defined by $V^O(p) = \{(h, t) \mid t \in V(p)\}$. Now, we define the following **translation from PBTL to OBTL**, recursively on PBTL-formulae, where $p \in \mathrm{PROP}$:

- $\tau(p) = \Box p$
- $\tau(\neg \phi) = \neg \tau(\phi)$
- $\tau(\phi \wedge \psi) = \tau(\phi) \wedge \tau(\psi)$
- $\tau(P\phi) = P\tau(\phi)$
- $\tau(H\phi) = H\tau(\phi)$
- $\tau(F\phi) = \Box F\tau(\phi)$
- $\tau(G\phi) = \Box G\tau(\phi)$
- $\tau(f\phi) = \Diamond F\tau(\phi)$
- $\tau(g\phi) = \Diamond G\tau(\phi)$

Now, for every PBTL-formula ϕ, a PBTL-model $\mathcal{M} = \langle T, <, V \rangle$ and $t \in T$:

$$\mathcal{M}, t \models \phi \text{ iff } \mathcal{M}^O, (h, t) \models \tau(\phi) \text{ for any } h \in \mathcal{H}(t)$$

This can be proved by an easy induction on the structure of PBTL-formulae.

On the other hand, PBTL is essentially less expressive than OBTL, as there is no Peircean formula which is equivalent to, for example, the Ockhamist $\Diamond \mathsf{GF} p$.

7.5 Full Computation Tree Logic CTL*

The full computation tree logic CTL* is the Ockhamist counterpart of the computation tree logic CTL presented in Section 6.4. More precisely, it is the Ockhamist logic in the language of OBTL extended with the temporal operators X and U, but without the past operators, and interpreted on ω-trees. This logic was introduced in response to the debate on the pros and cons of branching time vs linear time logics which took place in the early 1980s. These two logics are incomparable in their expressiveness and each has some computational advantages over the other: CTL has a much more efficient model-checking procedure than LTL (PTIME vs PSPACE), which in turn is more expressive than CTL for some important properties, such as fairness, while deciding its satisfiability appears to be somewhat easier than in the case of CTL (PSPACE vs EXPTIME). Thus, CTL* was proposed as a natural branching time logic subsuming both CTL and LTL, and being much more expressive than both, though having the same model-checking complexity as LTL and much higher complexity of deciding its satisfiability than both (2EXPTIME).

The standard language of CTL* contains the temporal operators of LTL, namely X, G, and U, plus the path quantifiers ∀ and ∃, which, unlike in CTL, can be freely combined and nested with the temporal operators. The standard semantics of CTL*, like that of CTL, is based on ω-trees, but the semantics here is Ockhamist, that is, truth of formulae is evaluated on a pair (ω-path, a position on it), which is equivalent to a branch on the path. That semantics is generalised to bundled trees, and to any (not only tree-like) serial Kripke models, representing transition systems, just like the semantics of CTL.

7.6 Axiomatic Systems for Ockhamist Validity

Several alternative versions of axiomatic systems have been proposed for OBTL for both Ockhamist validity and Ockhamist BT-validity.

I will first present an axiomatic system $\mathsf{Ax_{OBTL-BT}}$ for Ockhamist BT-validity with respect to the class of bundled trees[23] with irreflexive precedence,

---

[23] This is a variation of the sound and complete axiomatic system for Ockhamist BT-validity in Zanardo (1985), where the semantics is given in terms of what is called there 'Ockhamist frames', which are shown there to be semantically equivalent to bundled trees.

no beginning, and no end on any history, and with arbitrary Ockhamist valuations. Here is the list of axiom schemes:

(A0-A3) The axioms of the modal logic S5 for $\square$, namely:

(A0) A complete set of propositional tautologies.

(A1) $\square(\phi \to \psi) \to (\square\phi \to \square\psi)$

(A2) $\square\phi \to \phi$

(A3) $\Diamond\phi \to \square\Diamond\phi$

(A4–A10) The complete set of axiom schemes for the logic L_t of the class of all strict linear orderings, see Section 3.6.

(A11–A12) P⊤, F⊤.

(A13) $(P(\square p \wedge Gq) \wedge H\neg(q \wedge \Diamond r)) \to \square(Gp_1 \wedge Pr \to P(p \wedge (r \vee Pr) \wedge G(r \to Gp_1)))$.

(A14) $[Hp \wedge H\neg(q \wedge \Diamond r \wedge F(q \wedge p \wedge \Diamond r_1)) \wedge P(\square p_1 \wedge Gq)] \to$
$$\square(Gq_1 \to P(p_1 \wedge G(r \to G(r_1 \to Gq_1)))).$$

Checking the validity of the schemes (A1–A12) is a relatively routine task; the last two require some effort, mainly because their semantic intuition is not evident from the syntax. They essentially express correspondences between branches, and their precise meaning can best be extracted from their use in the completeness proof in Zanardo (1985), which the reader can inspect directly.

The inference rules of $Ax^{IB}_{OBTL-BT}$ involve the standard Modus Ponens $\square$-Necessitation, G-Necessitation, and H-Necessitation, as well as uniform substitution, unless the formulae A13 and A14 are replaced by schemes.

Now, I will present a somewhat simpler axiomatic system for Ockhamist BT-validity,[24] assuming that the atomic propositions are instant-based. That axiomatic system, denoted here by $Ax^{IB}_{OBTL-BT}$, extends the list of axiom schemes and inference rules for G and H for the logic L_t of linearly ordered time flows (cf. Section 3.6) with the following additional schemes for $\square$, capturing the interaction of $\square$ with the temporal operators on branching time models:

S5($\square$) The axioms of the modal logic S5 for $\square$, as in $Ax_{OBTL-BT}$.

(HN1) $p \to \square p$, for each (instant-based) atomic proposition p.

(HN2) $H\square\phi \to \square H\phi$, essentially saying that all histories through the current instant share the same past.

---

[24] This system was presented in Reynolds (2002), though the scheme HN2 is incorrectly given there as a biconditional. There is no completeness proof presented in that paper, but only a reference to proof details in Gabbay et al. (1994), where, however, a different axiomatisation is given.

(HN3) $P\square\phi \rightarrow \square P\phi$, essentially saying that all histories passing through the current instant also pass through any instant that is in the past of it.

(HN4) $\square G\phi \rightarrow G\square\phi$, essentially saying that all branches in the future are future 'sub-branches' of branches in the present.

(HN5) $G\perp \rightarrow \square G\perp$, following from maximality of histories: if the history containing the current branch ends at the current instant, then *every* history through that instant ends there, so one history cannot properly extend another.

Checking the soundness of these schemes is a fairly routine task.

The inference rules of $\text{Ax}^{\text{IB}}_{\text{OBTL–BT}}$ comprise Modus Ponens, $\square$-Necessitation, G-Necessitation, and H-Necessitation, and the following non-standard rule:

$$\textbf{(IRR)}: \quad \frac{(p \wedge H\neg p) \rightarrow \varphi}{\varphi}, \text{ assuming that } p \text{ does not occur in } \varphi.$$

We have already seen this rule in Section 6.3. Its intended role is the same here, mostly in the completeness proof. The argument that it preserves validity, now in OBTL-models, is very similar, except that the modification of the valuation of p in a falsifying model now is to make p true *only* at the current state.

In the quest to axiomatise the standard Ockhamist validity, Reynolds proposed to add the following infinite scheme of '*limit closure axioms*':

$$\textbf{(LC)} \quad \square G_{\leq} \bigwedge_{i=0}^{n-1}(\Diamond\varphi_i \rightarrow \Diamond F \Diamond \varphi_{i+1}) \rightarrow \Diamond G_{\leq} \bigwedge_{i=0}^{n-1}(\Diamond\varphi_i \rightarrow F \Diamond \varphi_{i+1})$$

where $\varphi_0, \ldots, \varphi_{n-1}$ are any OBTL formulae, $\varphi_n = \varphi_0$, and $G_{\leq}\theta := \theta \wedge G\theta$. However, the problem of proving completeness remains at present open.[25]

Still, the logic CTL* and its extension with past operators PCTL* have been completely axiomatised. For the quite elaborated completeness proofs, see Reynolds (2001) and Reynolds (2005).

7.7 Some Variations of Branching Time Semantics

A variation of the Ockhamist semantics was proposed by Nishimura (1979), where the models involve both sets of instants and sets of (disjoint) histories, both regarded as primary objects. These can be thought of as obtained by taking apart the histories in Ockhamist models. The semantics essentially only differs from the Ockhamist semantics in relativising the temporal operators to the current history of evaluation not only for the future, but also for the present and past. This apparently reflects a view of Leibniz, so it was named '*Leibnizian*

---

[25] A completeness proof was announced in Reynolds (2003) with a sketch of the proof argument, but no full completeness proof of which I am aware has been published yet.

Tense Logic' (LT) in Øhrstrøm and Hasle (1995). Still, in Leibnizian models every instant belongs to exactly one history, so in the Leibnizian semantics the truth-value of a formula only depends, as in the Peircean semantics, on the current instant. Notably, the validities in the two semantics differ: every LT-valid formula is OBTL-valid (which can be seen by a simple transformation of Ockhamist models to LT-models), but not vice versa. See an example in Braüner et al. (2000).

Another interesting variation of the Ockhamist models and semantics was proposed in to Belnap and Green (1994), where they argue against the Ockhamist notion of an 'actual future', which they call the '*Thin Red Line*'. They find it problematic and claim that 'one can make sense of an indeterministic, branching structure for our world without postulating an actual future as distinguished among the possibilities, instead promoting the idea of an "open future"'. Further, Belnap and Green (1994) propose a solution to the problem they identify by arguing that not only the true actual future on the history through the (currently considered) actual instant must be specified in the model and taken into account in the evaluation of formulae, but also, for every alternative instant, the future stemming from that instant and designated as the 'true future' there. This is needed for counterfactual reasoning about truth in possible and necessary futures, which cannot be adequately formalised in the Ockhamist semantics. That leads to the idea (which can be traced back to the sixteenth-century scholar Luis de Molina) of defining the Thin Red Line as a function TRL, fixed in the model, which assigns to every instant in the model a history passing through that instant and representing the future which would presumably evolve from that instant if it is the actual one. This results in an instant-based semantics, with modified semantic clauses for the future operators:

- $\mathcal{M}, t \models F\phi$ iff $\mathcal{M}, t' \models \phi$ for some instant $t' \in \mathrm{TRL}(t)$ such that $t < t'$.
- $\mathcal{M}, t \models G\phi$ iff $\mathcal{M}, t' \models \phi$ for every instant $t' \in \mathrm{TRL}(t)$ such that $t < t'$.

The semantics of past operators is as the Peircean semantics in tree-like models.

The function TRL must satisfy some natural conditions,[26] including:

(TRL1) $t \in \mathrm{TRL}(t)$ for every instant t.
(TRL2) If $t < t'$ and $t' \in \mathrm{TRL}(t)$ then $\mathrm{TRL}(t') = \mathrm{TRL}(t)$, for every t, t'.

The TRL function defines a bundle of 'designated/preferred' histories in the model and thus enables semantics of the type based on bundled trees, as in

---

[26] The condition (TRL2) is an improved version of the original condition from Belnap and Green (1994), proposed in Øhrstrøm and Hasle (1995).

Section 7.3.3. Still, that semantics is somewhat more general and some BT-validities of OBTL are not valid in the TRL-based semantics without imposing additional conditions on TRL. An example of such non-validity is $q \to PFq$, because the current instant need not belong to the designated history passing through any past instant. See more on TRL theories in Øhrstrøm (2014).

Zanardo (1998) develops a new semantics for branching time logic, based on trees endowed with an 'indistinguishability function', assigning to every instant a local indistinguishability relation on the histories passing through that instant, and generalising both the Peircean and the Ockhamist semantics.

Another, more recent generalisation of the idea of branching time structures is the *transition semantics* proposed in Rumberg (2016), where the possible histories (courses of events) are successively built up from local future possibilities and viewed as (possibly non-maximal) chains of local transitions.

There is much more to say about these and other variations of branching time models, semantics, and logics than the space here allows. For more, I direct the reader to the references mentioned in this section.

7.8 Aristotle's 'Sea-Battle Tomorow' Revisited in Branching Time Models

Much of the early development of branching time models and logics was driven by attempts to formally resolve the problems arising from logical treatment of *future contingents*, most notably Aristotle's 'Sea-battle tomorrow': what, if any, should be the present truth value of the contingent statement

Q = '*There will be a sea-battle tomorrow*'?

According to Aristotle, the principle of bivalence still applies: either there will be a sea-battle tomorrow or there will not be one, though we just do not know which will be the case, so we cannot assign the truth values today. Łukasiewicz proposed a stronger solution, namely, that the truth value assigned to Q today should be neither true nor false, but a third truth value, *undetermined* (or, *undefined*). With this motivation Łukasiewicz introduced his 3-valued logic, where if p is undetermined then $\neg p$ is also undetermined, and therefore $p \vee \neg p$ is undetermined, too.

Now, let us look at the possible solutions that branching time semantics offer. First, since Q is a future contingent, it is true in some possible futures and false in others. Here are several options for its truth value, depending on the adopted semantics of branching time, where X refers to tomorrow:

- *Ockhamist*: exactly one future is true (actual), but we do not know which one. Thus, in an Ockhamist model $XQ \wedge X\neg Q$ is false, but $XQ \vee X\neg Q$ is true.

Further, suppose that no sea-battle occurs in the actual future.
Then, $\neg XQ \wedge X\neg Q$ is true (though, not presently known).

- Similarly, in Nishimura's (Leibnizian) semantics and in semantics involving the Thin Red Line, the truth of Q is determined by the actual (respectively, the designated) history, passing through the current instant.
- *Peircean*: In Peircean models there is no actual future yet, just some possible futures. Thus, neither XQ nor $X\neg Q$ is true now, so $XQ \vee X\neg Q$ is false.
- *Kripkean*: According to Kripke, both XQ and $X\neg Q$ are true. (Here X behaves like the Peircean weak future operator f.)

Another formal logical approach to resolving the 'sea-battle tomorrow' problem is proposed in Ju, Grilletti, and Goranko (2018) by invalidating the argument leading to the fatalistic conclusion that whether there will be a sea-battle tomorrow or not, the outcome is necessarily the case already now.

Some References

For further readings related to the Ockhamist branching time logic OBTL, CTL* and other variations of it, see Prior (1967, ch. 7.4), Gabbay (1973), Gabbay (1975), Burgess (1978), Burgess (1980), Nishimura (1979), Thomason (1984), Emerson and Halpern (1985), Gurevich and Shelah (1985), Zanardo (1985), Emerson (1990), Stirling (1992), Belnap and Green (1994), Gabbay et al. (1994), Zanardo (1996), Zanardo (1998), Belnap, Perloff, and Xu (2001), Reynolds (2001), Reynolds (2002), Reynolds (2003), Reynolds (2005), Demri et al. (2016), Ju et al. (2018), Florio and Frigerio (2020), Santelli (2022).

8 First-Order Temporal Logics

Objects exist in time and their properties change over time. Propositional temporal logics are not expressive enough to capture the richness and dynamics of the world, as all that is associated with an instant in a model of propositional temporal logic is a set of abstract atomic propositions that are just declared true there. What is needed, instead, is a full-fledged model of the temporal history of the world, with objects that may have certain properties and stand in certain relations. Accordingly, the language should contain names for objects, variables and quantifiers ranging over objects, as well as predicates for denoting properties and relations, to adequately describe how the world is at a given instant in time – in addition to temporal operators for reasoning about how the world changes over time. This is what first-order temporal logics provide.

8.1 Existence and Quantification in Time

Existence in time is a major topic in the philosophy of time. Usually, objects come into being at one point in time and go out of being at some later time. But, what does it mean for an object to exist in time? Do only present objects exist, as a *presentist* would argue, or is existence to be understood in a broader sense, comprising past and future objects as well, as an *eternalist* would hold? The controversy between *presentism* and *eternalism* is accompanied by a debate on *persistence*, that is, on the question of how objects exist *through time*: are objects wholly present at each instant at which they exist or do they persist by having different states of existence at different instants in time?

Similar questions concerning the existence of objects in time and their identity over time arise in the formal context of first-order temporal logics, albeit under a different guise. These questions become particularly important when it comes to the interaction of temporality and quantification. For example, the sentence[27] '*A philosopher will be a king*' can be interpreted and formalised in first-order temporal logic in several different ways:

- $\exists x(\text{philosopher}(x) \wedge \text{F king}(x))$
  Someone who is now a philosopher will be a king at some future time.
- $\exists x \text{F}(\text{philosopher}(x) \wedge \text{king}(x))$
  There now exists someone who will at some future time be both a philosopher and a king.
- $\text{F}\exists x(\text{philosopher}(x) \wedge \text{F king}(x))$
  There will exist someone who is a philosopher and later will be a king.
- $\text{F}\exists x(\text{philosopher}(x) \wedge \text{king}(x))$
  There will exist someone who is at the same time a philosopher and a king.

These interpretations assume that the domain of quantification is always relative to an instant and that the same individual may exist at different instants. To enable these interpretations, one has to introduce in our models a *local domain* of objects $D(t)$ for each instant t, to restrict the range of the quantifiers to that domain, and to identify the same object across different times.

Moreover, this example suggests that the local domain at a given instant contains exactly those individuals that do, in fact, exist at that instant. From a logical point of view, however, there are alternative ways to think of the local domains associated with instants, which mirror different conceptions of existence in time. Here are four natural options:

---

[27] I have borrowed this example from the 2008 version of the SEP entry on temporal logic by Anthony Galton.

1. Objects come into being at one point in time and go out of being at a later time, that is, they actually exist only over a certain period of time. This idea can be formally captured by assuming that the local domain at a given instant comprises those, and only those, objects that *presently exist* at that instant. Thus, objects belong to the local domains of precisely those instants at which they actually exist, so *the local domains vary over time*. In this sense, the sentences '*Every (existing) human was born after 1888*' and '*Every (existing) human will die before 2220*' are currently (in all likelihood) true.

2. Objects actually exist over a period of time, but they remain in the temporal history of the world once they have ceased to actually exist. On this account, the local domain at an instant includes not only those objects that presently exist, but all past objects, as well. That is, *the local domains increase* as time progresses and new objects come into being. In this sense, '*Socrates and I exist and will always exist*' is true, while '*Every (existing) human was born after 1888*' is false.

3. Alternatively, one may hold that all objects that will ever exist are initially part of the temporal history of the world but drop out once they have ceased to actually exist. Technically, this amounts to the idea that the local domain at an instant comprises all present and future objects. Thus, *the local domains decrease* as time progresses and objects go out of being. In this sense, '*Socrates existed, but will never exist again*' is true, while '*Every human will die before 2220*' is (hopefully) false.

4. Past, present, and future objects exist on a par. This is the notion of existence in an eternalist sense. One way to formally capture this idea is by requiring that the local domain associated with an instant contains all objects in the entire temporal history of the world. Hence, *the local domains remain constant over time*. Here, '*Socrates exists, and so does his mother, as well as every present or future descendant of the current king of Sweden*' is true.

A conceptually different but technically closely related issue concerns the scope of quantification. What do we quantify over in a temporal setting:

- over all present, past, and future objects in the temporal history of the world?
- or, only over those objects that presently exist at the current instant?

Adapting the terminology 'possibilist quantification' and 'actualist quantification' from Fitting and Mendelsohn (1998) to the temporal case, we may refer to the former kind of quantification as *eternalist quantification* and use the term *presentist quantification* for the latter.

A further issue arising here concerns fictitious entities, such as Pegasus, Santa Claus, Superman, Pippi Longstocking, and so on, which do not actually exist at any instant. Still, they may be said to exist in some broader sense (as fictitious individuals), and one may want to include them in the domain of quantification. A version of classical first-order logic, called *Free Logic* allows handling of non-existing entities, but this will not be discussed further here.

8.2 Preliminaries: First-Order Relational Structures and Languages

This is a short summary of basics of classical first-order logic used further. Readers familiar with this material can skip this summary.

A **first-order relational structure** consists of:

- a non-empty set of objects D, called the **domain (of discourse)**,
- designated **objects**, or **individuals**, in D denoted by **constants**,
- designated **relations** in D denoted by *predicates*.

I will only discuss purely relational structures with constants here, but will not consider structures with designated functions.

Here are two natural examples of first-order relational structures:

- the numerical structure N with a domain being the set of natural numbers $\mathbb{N}$, the relations $=$ and $<$, and the designated object 0.
- the structure H with a domain being the set of all (ever existing) humans with unary relations (i.e., properties) like *man* and *woman*, binary relations like *parent of*, *child of*, and *loves*, and designated individuals *Adam*, *Eve*, *Joe*, *Mia*, and so on.

The vocabulary of a relational first-order language $\mathcal{L}$ comprises:

- **Non-logical symbols: constants:** $a, b, c, \ldots$; **predicates** (of specified arities): $Q, R, \ldots$; and **individual variables:** $x, y, z, \ldots$.
  The non-logical symbols determine the **signature** of the language.
- **Logical symbols: truth-functional connectives:** $\neg, \wedge, \vee, \rightarrow, \leftrightarrow$; **equality:** $=$; **quantifiers:** $\forall, \exists$; **auxiliary symbols:** $(\,,)\,,\, ,$.

Terms in $\mathcal{L}$ are constant symbols and individual variables. **Atomic formulae** in $\mathcal{L}$ are of the form $R(\tau_1, \ldots, \tau_n)$, where $\tau_1, \ldots, \tau_n$ are terms in $\mathcal{L}$ and R is an n-ary predicate symbol in $\mathcal{L}$. In particular, $\tau_1 = \tau_2$ is an atomic formula. The set of **formulae** of $\mathcal{L}$ is inductively defined, as usual. We distinguish between **bound** or **free** occurrences of variables in formulae, depending on whether or not the variable occurs in the scope of a quantifier binding that variable.

Closed formulae (not containing any free occurrences of variables) are called **sentences**. For more background on first-order logic, see for example, Fitting and Mendelsohn (1998), Hodges (2001), Halbach (2010), or Goranko (2016).

8.3 The Language and Models of FOTL

The basic language of first-order temporal logic (FOTL) is essentially an extension of a first-order language with Prior's temporal operators P and F. Whereas atomic propositions in propositional temporal logics are unstructured entities, atomic formulae in first-order temporal logics are built up from terms (denoting individuals) and predicate symbols (denoting relations). Besides, the language is equipped with quantifiers ranging over individuals. In what follows, I will consider FOTL over a relational first-order language with constants (but no function symbols) and equality. The set of formulae is defined as follows:

$$\varphi := R(\tau_1, \ldots, \tau_n) \mid \tau_1 = \tau_2 \mid \bot \mid \neg\varphi \mid (\varphi \wedge \varphi) \mid \forall x \varphi \mid \mathsf{H}\varphi \mid \mathsf{G}\varphi,$$

where $R(\tau_1, \ldots, \tau_n)$ and $\tau_1 = \tau_2$ are atomic formulae. The truth-functional connectives $\vee$, $\rightarrow$, and $\leftrightarrow$, as well as the weak temporal operators P and F, are defined as usual.[28] Also, the dual $\exists$ of $\forall$ is defined by $\exists x \varphi := \neg\forall x \neg\varphi$.

The models of FOTL are based on temporal frames where each instant is associated with a first-order relational structure, with the same signature in all instants. Formally, a **first-order temporal model** (FOTM) is a quintuple $\mathcal{M} = (T, <, \mathcal{D}, \mathrm{Dom}, \mathcal{I})$, where:

- $\mathcal{T} = \langle T, < \rangle$ is a temporal frame,
- $\mathcal{D}$ is the **global domain (universe)** of the model,
- $\mathrm{Dom} : T \rightarrow \mathcal{P}(\mathcal{D})$ is a **domain function**, assigning to each instant $t \in T$ a **local domain** $\mathrm{Dom}_t \subseteq \mathcal{D}$.[29]
- $\mathcal{I}$ is an **interpretation function**, assigning for each $t \in T$:
  - an object $\mathcal{I}_t(c) \in \mathcal{D}$ to each constant symbol c,
  - an n-ary relation $\mathcal{I}_t(R) \subseteq \mathcal{D}^n$ to each n-ary predicate symbol R.

Note that the interpretations of the constant and predicate symbols are defined locally, that is, with respect to a given instant, whereas the respective extensions range over the global domain. This approach allows for reference

---

[28] Here I choose to consider the strong temporal operators as primitives and the weak ones as definable. This has some technical advantage in the axiomatic systems.

[29] Note that I do not require that $\mathcal{D} = \bigcup_{t \in T} \mathrm{Dom}_t$. Such an assumption implicitly excludes the possibility of referring to fictitious individuals that do not actually exist at any instant. The problem can be alternatively resolved by including such fictitious individuals in the local domains, thus also considering larger "external" local domains.

to objects that do not currently exist and enables a proper treatment of cross-temporal relations, as, for example, in the sentences '*Socrates hated his wife*', '*C. S. Pierce had a longer beard than Aristotle*', or '*Every nineteenth-century philosopher had studied the works of some student of Plato*'. On the other hand, the local interpretation of constant and predicate symbols creates the problems of *identity and persistence of properties over time*, that is, how to ensure that the interpretations of 'Socrates' back in the year 399 BC and now are the same, or that $2 < 3$ always means the same. These problems are inherent in first-order temporal logics and I will partly discuss them further.

The quadruple $\mathcal{F} = (T, <, \mathcal{D}, \text{Dom})$ will be called the **augmented temporal frame** of the model $\mathcal{M}$. Since the model is supposed to represent the temporal evolution of the world, the local domains at the different instants in the underlying augmented temporal frame must be suitably connected. There are four basic natural cases to distinguish for an augmented temporal frame, respectively for any first-order temporal model based on it:

1. **varying domains**: no restrictions apply[30].
2. **expanding (increasing) domains**:
   for all $t, t' \in T$, if $t < t'$, then $\text{Dom}_t \subseteq \text{Dom}_{t'}$;
3. **shrinking (decreasing) domains**:
   for all $t, t' \in T$, if $t < t'$, then $\text{Dom}_{t'} \subseteq \text{Dom}_t$;
4. **locally constant domains**:
   for all $t, t' \in T$, if $t < t'$ then, $\text{Dom}_t = \text{Dom}_{t'}$.
   Thus, an augmented temporal frame $\mathcal{F}$ has locally constant domains if and only if it has both expanding and shrinking domains. In particular, we say that $\mathcal{F}$ has a **constant domain** if all local domains are the same as the global domain. When the set of instants is temporally connected (i.e., every instant can be reached in finitely many forward or backward steps along the precedence relation), locally constant domains which are equal to the global domain imply a constant domain.

One can naturally relate the four cases distinguished here with the four respective notions of existence in time discussed earlier, in Section 8.1.

8.4 Semantics of FOTL

Formulae of FOTL are evaluated in first-order temporal models locally at instants. However, since the formulae of FOTL may contain variables, the

---

[30] A special case of varying domains, which will not be discussed further, would have the constraint that if an object c is in Dom_t and also in $\text{Dom}_{t'}$, then c is in Dom_t for every t such that $t < t < t'$, that is, that objects exist in some continuous (or, uninterrupted) stretch of time.

notion of truth is relativised not only to a model and an instant, but also to an assignment of individuals as values of the individual variables. I will denote the set of individual variables of an arbitrarily fixed language of FOTL by VAR and the set of its individual terms (i.e., variables and constants) by TERM.

8.4.1 Variable Assignments and Truth of FOTL Formulae

Given a first-order temporal model $\mathcal{M} = (T, <, \mathcal{D}, \text{Dom}, \mathcal{I})$, a **variable assignment** in $\mathcal{M}$ is a mapping $v : \text{VAR} \to \mathcal{D}$ that assigns to each $x \in \text{VAR}$ an element $v(x)$ in the global domain $\mathcal{D}$ of the model. Each such assignment v can be uniquely extended to a **term valuation** $\bar{v} : T \times \text{TERM} \to \mathcal{D}$ as follows:
$$\bar{v}(t, x) := v(x), \quad \bar{v}(t, c) := \mathcal{I}_t(c).$$

Note that the variable assignment is defined globally, whereas the valuation of the constant symbols depends on the respective instant.

The **truth of a formula φ of FOTL in a first-order temporal model $\mathcal{M}$, at an instant t, with respect to a variable assignment v**, denoted $\mathcal{M}, t \models_v \varphi$, is now defined recursively as follows:

- $\mathcal{M}, t \models_v R(\tau_1, \ldots, \tau_n)$ iff $(\bar{v}(t, \tau_1), \ldots, \bar{v}(t, \tau_n)) \in \mathcal{I}_t(R)$,
  for any n-ary predicate symbol R and terms $\tau_1, \ldots, \tau_n \in \text{TERM}$.
  Intuitively: $R(\tau_1, \ldots, \tau_n)$ is true with respect to v at the instant t if the tuple of individuals $(\bar{v}(t, \tau_1), \ldots, \bar{v}(t, \tau_n))$ designated by (i.e., assigned as values by v to) the terms $\tau_1, \ldots, \tau_n$ in t has the property $\mathcal{I}_t(R)$ designated by R at t, that is, belongs to the extension of the predicate R at t in $\mathcal{M}$.
- $\mathcal{M}, t \models_v \tau_1 = \tau_2$ iff $\bar{v}(t, \tau_1) = \bar{v}(t, \tau_2)$, for any terms $\tau_1, \tau_2 \in \text{TERM}$;
- $\mathcal{M}, t \not\models_v \bot$; $\mathcal{M}, t \models_v \neg\varphi$ iff $\mathcal{M}, t \not\models_v \varphi$;
- $\mathcal{M}, t \models_v \varphi \wedge \psi$ iff $\mathcal{M}, t \models_v \varphi$ and $\mathcal{M}, t \models_v \psi$;
- $\mathcal{M}, t \models_v \mathsf{H}\varphi$ iff $\mathcal{M}, t' \models_v \varphi$ for all $t' \in T$ such that $t' < t$;
- $\mathcal{M}, t \models_v \mathsf{G}\varphi$ iff $\mathcal{M}, t' \models_v \varphi$ for all $t' \in T$ such that $t < t'$;
- $\mathcal{M}, t \models_v \forall x \varphi$ iff ...
  - **presentist quantification**: ...$\mathcal{M}, t \models_{v[a/x]} \varphi$ for every $a \in \text{Dom}_t$;
  - **eternalist quantification**: ...$\mathcal{M}, t \models_{v[a/x]} \varphi$ for every $a \in \mathcal{D}$,
  where $v[a/x]$ is the variant of the assignment v such that $v[a/x](x) = a$.

So, $\forall x \varphi$ is true for v at t iff φ is true at t for each reassignment of value to x:

- *in the global domain $\mathcal{D}$*, in the eternalist semantics,
- respectively, only *in the local domain* Dom_t, in the presentist semantics.

Therefore, the presentist quantification amounts to quantification over the *local* domain at the given instant, whereas the eternalist quantification is construed as quantification over the *global* domain.

The derived semantic clauses for P, F, and ∃ respectively read as follows:

- $\mathcal{M}, t \models_v \mathsf{P}\varphi$ iff $\mathcal{M}, t' \models_v \varphi$ for some $t' \in T$ such that $t' \prec t$;
- $\mathcal{M}, t \models_v \mathsf{F}\varphi$ iff $\mathcal{M}, t' \models_v \varphi$ for some $t' \in T$ such that $t \prec t'$;
- $\mathcal{M}, t \models_v \exists x\varphi$ iff ...
  - *presentist quantification*: ...$\mathcal{M}, t \models_{v[a/x]} \varphi$ for some $a \in \mathrm{Dom}_t$;
  - *eternalist quantification*: ...$\mathcal{M}, t \models_{v[a/x]} \varphi$ for some $a \in \mathcal{D}$.

8.4.2 Varying and Constant Domain Semantics

Note that the presentist quantification naturally relates to first-order temporal models with varying domains, while in the semantics based on eternalist quantification the local domains do not play any essential role. In fact, from a technical point of view, eternalist quantification amounts to the assumption that the model has a constant domain, that is, all local domains equal the global domain. Moreover, in constant domain models the semantics based on presentist quantification coincides with the semantics based on eternalist quantification. Thus, presentist quantification suggests a **varying domain semantics**, which we can also call **presentist semantics**, whereas the semantics associated with eternalist quantification is a **constant domain semantics**, which we can also call **eternalist semantics**. In what follows I will use these expressions interchangeably.

In each of these semantics, a FOTL formula φ is said to be **valid in a model** $\mathcal{M}$ iff it is true in that model at each instant with respect to every variable assignment; it is **valid in an augmented temporal frame** iff it is valid in each model based on that frame; and it is **valid** iff it is valid in every model.

Adopting one or the other approach to quantification affects the notion of validity, even for non-temporal principles. For instance, the sentence $\exists x(x = c)$ is valid in FOL. It is valid in constant domain semantics, as well, but it is no longer valid in varying domain semantics, because the object assigned to the constant c may not belong to the local domain. Another principle from plain first-order logic that distinguishes the two semantics is the scheme of *Universal Instantiation*: $\forall x\varphi(x) \rightarrow \varphi(\tau)$, which is, likewise, valid in constant domain semantics but invalid in varying domain semantics, for analogous reasons.

8.4.3 Temporal Barcan Formulae

The main distinction between varying domain and the constant domain semantics is in the validity of some principles that express important patterns of interaction between temporal operators and quantification, most notably including the *Barcan formula schemes* and their converses. These are named after the philosopher and logician Ruth Marcus Barcan, who studied them in the context of first-order modal logic in her 1946 doctoral thesis. Here are the FOTL versions[31] of these formulae:

– **Future Barcan Formula** scheme: $(\mathrm{BF_G})\ \forall x G\varphi(x) \to G\forall x\varphi(x).$

Equivalent[32] existential version: $(\mathrm{BF_F})\ \mathsf{F}\exists x\varphi(x) \to \exists x \mathsf{F}\varphi(x).$

– **Converse Future Barcan Formula** scheme: $(\mathrm{CBF_G})\ G\forall x\varphi(x) \to \forall x G\varphi(x).$

Equivalent existential version: $(\mathrm{CBF_F})\ \exists x \mathsf{F}\varphi(x) \to \mathsf{F}\exists x\varphi(x).$

– **Past Barcan Formula** scheme: $(\mathrm{BF_H})\ \forall x H\varphi(x) \to H\forall x\varphi(x).$

Equivalent existential version: $(\mathrm{BF_P})\ \mathsf{P}\exists x\varphi(x) \to \exists x \mathsf{P}\varphi(x).$

– **Converse Past Barcan Formula** scheme: $(\mathrm{CBF_H})\ H\forall x\varphi(x) \to \forall x H\varphi(x).$

Equivalent existential version: $(\mathrm{CBF_P})\ \exists x \mathsf{P}\varphi(x) \to \mathsf{P}\exists x\varphi(x).$

In the following two subsections, we take a closer look at these and other important validities and non-validities in the respective semantics.

8.5 Eternalist Quantification and Constant Domain Semantics

Let us first explore FOTL validity in the constant domain (eternalist) semantics. Validity in that semantics will be denoted by $\models_{\mathrm{CD}}$.

8.5.1 On Validities and Non-validities in Constant Domain Semantics

Here are some validities in constant domain semantics, hereafter called CD-validities, and non-validities in that semantics.

1. All FOTL instances of valid first-order formulae are CD-valid.
2. In particular, the scheme of Universal Instantiation is CD-valid:
   $\models_{\mathrm{CD}} \forall x\varphi(x) \to \varphi(\tau)$, for any[33] term τ.
3. The Future Barcan Formula scheme, $\mathrm{BF_G}$, is CD-valid:
   $\models_{\mathrm{CD}} \forall x G\varphi(x) \to G\forall x\varphi(x)$ or, equivalently, $\models_{\mathrm{CD}} \mathsf{F}\exists x\varphi(x) \to \exists x \mathsf{F}\varphi(x).$
   To prove the first validity, take a FOTL model $\mathcal{M} = (T, <, \mathcal{D}, \mathrm{Dom}, \mathcal{I})$, variable assignment v in $\mathcal{M}$, and instant $t \in T$. Suppose $\mathcal{M}, t \models_v \forall x G\varphi(x)$. Then

---

[31] Here I adopt the terminology of McArthur (1976, ch. 4).

[32] The equivalence is by contraposition. In fact, this is the version that corresponds to the modal Barcan formula as it originally appeared in Barcan (1946), but the prevailing tradition since then, which I follow here, was to adopt the universal version.

[33] In languages with function symbols the term τ must be free for substitution for x in φ.

$M, t \models_{v[a/x]} G\varphi(x)$, for every $a \in \mathcal{D}$. Hence, $M, s \models_{v[a/x]} \varphi(x)$, for every $a \in \mathcal{D}$ and $s > t$. Then, $M, s \models_v \forall x\varphi(x)$, for every $s > t$.

Therefore, $M, s \models_v G\forall x\varphi(x)$. Thus, $M, t \models_v \forall x G\varphi(x) \rightarrow G\forall x\varphi(x)$.

4. The Converse Future Barcan Formula scheme, $\mathrm{CBF_G}$, is CD-valid:
   $\models_{\mathrm{CD}} G\forall x\varphi(x) \rightarrow \forall x G\varphi(x)$ or, equivalently, $\models_{\mathrm{CD}} \exists x F\varphi(x) \rightarrow F\exists x\varphi(x)$.
   The proof is fully analogous to the previous one.

5. Some important non-validities include:
   $\not\models_{\mathrm{CD}} G\exists x\varphi(x) \rightarrow \exists x G\varphi(x)$ and, equivalently, $\not\models_{\mathrm{CD}} \forall x F\varphi(x) \rightarrow F\forall x\varphi(x)$.
   It suffices to show this when $\varphi(x) = Q(x)$, for a unary predicate Q.
   A counter-model for the first formula is $M = (T, <, \mathcal{D}, \mathrm{Dom}, I)$, where $T = \{s, t\}$, $< = \{(s, s), (s, t), (t, t)\}$, $\mathcal{D} = \{a, b\}$, $I_s(Q) = \{a\}$ and $I_t(Q) = \{b\}$.
   For any assignment v in M: $M, s \models_v G\exists x Q(x)$, because $M, s \models_v \exists x Q(x)$ and $M, t \models_v \exists x Q(x)$, but $M, s \not\models_v \exists x G Q(x)$ because $I_s(Q) \cap I_t(Q) = \emptyset$.

Analogous claims hold for the past versions of the aforementioned schemes, with H and P instead of G and F.

8.5.2 An Axiomatic System for the Eternalist Semantics

Here is an axiomatic system **FOTL(CD)** for all CD-validities.

I. *Axiom schemes:*

1. All axioms of the minimal propositional temporal logic $\mathbf{K}_t$.
2. Universal Instantiation ($\forall$-Elimination):
   $\forall x\varphi(x) \rightarrow \varphi(\tau)$, for any term τ (free for substitution for x in φ).
3. Reflexivity of equality: $\forall x(x = x)$.
4. Extensionality: $\forall x\forall y(x = y \rightarrow (\varphi[x/z] \rightarrow \varphi[y/z]))$.
5. Future necessity of non-equality: $\forall x\forall y(x \neq y \rightarrow G(x \neq y))$.

II. *Inference rules* (where $\vdash_{\mathrm{CD}}$ denotes derivability in **FOTL(CD)**):

1. Modus Ponens: If $\vdash_{\mathrm{CD}} \varphi \rightarrow \psi$ and $\vdash_{\mathrm{CD}} \varphi$, then $\vdash_{\mathrm{CD}} \psi$.
2. G-Necessitation: If $\vdash_{\mathrm{CD}} \varphi$, then $\vdash_{\mathrm{CD}} G\varphi$.
3. H-Necessitation: If $\vdash_{\mathrm{CD}} \varphi$, then $\vdash_{\mathrm{CD}} H\varphi$.
4. Universal Generalisation ($\forall$-Introduction):
   If $\vdash_{\mathrm{CD}} \psi \rightarrow \varphi(x)$, then $\vdash_{\mathrm{CD}} \psi \rightarrow \forall x\varphi$, where x does not occur free in ψ.

Some important theorems of **FOTL(CD)**:

1. Symmetry of equality: $\vdash_{\mathrm{CD}} \forall x\forall y(x = y \rightarrow y = x)$.
   [Derived from Extensionality, applied to $\varphi := (z = x)$.]

2. Future necessity of equality: $\vdash_{CD} \forall x \forall y(x = y \rightarrow G(x = y))$.
   [Derived from Extensionality, applied to $\varphi := G(x = z)$.]
3. Past necessity of equality: $\vdash_{CD} \forall x \forall y(x = y \rightarrow H(x = y))$.
   [Derived likewise.]
4. Past necessity of non-equality: $\forall x \forall y(x \neq y \rightarrow H(x \neq y))$.
   [Derived from the future necessity of equality.]
5. Transitivity of equality: $\vdash_{CD} \forall x \forall y \forall z(x = y \wedge y = z \rightarrow x = z)$.
6. The Converse Future Barcan formula CBF$_G$: $\vdash_{CD} G\forall x\varphi(x) \rightarrow \forall x G\varphi(x)$.
   The derivation is very simple:

   (a) $\vdash_{CD} \forall x\varphi(x) \rightarrow \varphi(x)$ (Universal Instantiation)
   (b) $\vdash_{CD} G\forall x\varphi(x) \rightarrow G\varphi(x)$ (From (a) by NEC$_G$, K$_G$, MP)
   (c) $\vdash_{CD} G\forall x\varphi(x) \rightarrow \forall x G\varphi(x)$ (From (b) by Univ. Generalisation)

7. The Converse Past Barcan formula CBF$_H$: $\vdash_{CD} H\forall x\varphi(x) \rightarrow \forall x H\varphi(x)$
   [Derived by replacing G with H in the proof above.]
8. $\vdash_{CD} P\forall x\varphi(x) \rightarrow \forall x P\varphi(x)$. Here is a derivation:

   (a) $\vdash_{CD} \forall x\varphi(x) \rightarrow \varphi(x)$ (Universal Instantiation)
   (b) $\vdash_{CD} H(\forall x\varphi(x) \rightarrow \varphi(x))$ (From (a) by NEC$_H$)
   (c) $\vdash_{CD} H(\forall x\varphi(x) \rightarrow \varphi(x)) \rightarrow (P\forall x\varphi(x) \rightarrow P\varphi(x))$ (a case of TL validity)
   (d) $\vdash_{CD} P\forall x\varphi(x) \rightarrow P\varphi(x)$ (From (b) and (c) by MP)
   (e) $\vdash_{CD} P\forall x\varphi(x) \rightarrow \forall x P\varphi(x)$ (From (d) by Universal Generalisation)

9. The Future Barcan formula BF$_G$: $\vdash_{CD} \forall x G\varphi(x) \rightarrow G\forall x\varphi(x)$
   This derivation is not entirely trivial. Here is a sketch, omitting the more routine steps, done in classical logic:

   (a) $\vdash_{CD} PG\varphi(x) \rightarrow \varphi(x)$ (Instance of a TL validity)
   (b) $\vdash_{CD} \forall x PG\varphi(x) \rightarrow PG\varphi(x)$ (Universal Instantiation)
   (c) $\vdash_{CD} \forall x PG\varphi(x) \rightarrow \varphi(x)$ (From (a) and (b) by prop. logic)
   (d) $\vdash_{CD} P\forall x G\varphi(x) \rightarrow \forall x PG\varphi(x)$ (Instance of Theorem 8 above)
   (e) $\vdash_{CD} P\forall x G\varphi(x) \rightarrow \varphi(x)$ (From (c) and (d) by prop. logic)
   (f) $\vdash_{CD} P\forall x G\varphi(x) \rightarrow \forall x\varphi(x)$ (From (e) by Universal Generalisation)
   (g) $\vdash_{CD} GP\forall x G\varphi(x) \rightarrow G\forall x\varphi(x)$ (From (f) by NEC$_G$, K$_G$, MP)
   (h) $\vdash_{CD} \forall x G\varphi(x) \rightarrow GP\forall x G\varphi(x)$ (Instance of a TL validity)
   (i) $\vdash_{CD} \forall x G\varphi(x) \rightarrow G\forall x\varphi(x)$ (From (g) and (h) by prop. logic)

10. The Past Barcan formula BF$_H$: $\vdash_{CD} \forall x H\varphi(x) \rightarrow H\forall x\varphi(x)$.
    [Derived by replacing P and G with F and H in the proof in (9).]

8.6 Presentist Quantification and Varying Domain Semantics

In varying domain semantics, free variables range over the global domain, whereas quantifiers have a presentist reading and quantify over the local domains only. Consequently, some formulae that are CD-valid are no longer valid in varying domain semantics. Most importantly, varying domain semantics invalidates Universal Instantiation scheme $\forall x \varphi(x) \rightarrow \varphi(\tau)$, as well as both the Future and Past Barcan Formula schemes and their converses. To preserve all validities of FOL in the varying domains semantics of FOML, the condition of increasing domains is often assumed by default, but I will not make that default assumption here.

8.6.1 The Barcan Formulae and Varying Domain Semantics

The Barcan formulae schemes BF_G and BF_H and their converses CBF_G and CBF_H semantically correspond to conditions on the local domains that we have already seen. For any augmented temporal frame $\mathcal{F}$, the following holds, where $\models_{VD}$ denotes validity in the varying domain semantics:

1. $\mathcal{F}$ *has expanding domains iff* $\mathcal{F} \models_{VD} BF_H$ *iff* $\mathcal{F} \models_{VD} CBF_G$.
2. $\mathcal{F}$ *has shrinking domains iff* $\mathcal{F} \models_{VD} BF_G$ *iff* $\mathcal{F} \models_{VD} CBF_H$.

These two claims mirror each other with respect to the past-future reflection, so it suffices to prove the first one.

Proof: First, suppose $\mathcal{F} = (T, <, \mathcal{D}, \mathrm{Dom})$ has expanding domains.

To show that $\mathcal{F} \models_{VD} BF_H$, let us consider its equivalent existential version: $P\exists x \varphi(x) \rightarrow \exists x P \varphi(x)$. Take any FOTL model $\mathcal{M} = (T, <, \mathcal{D}, \mathrm{Dom}, \mathcal{I})$ on $\mathcal{F}$, a variable assignment v in $\mathcal{M}$, and $t \in T$. Suppose $\mathcal{M}, t \models_v P\exists x \varphi(x)$. Then $\mathcal{M}, s \models_v \exists x \varphi(x)$ for some $s < t$. Then, $\mathcal{M}, s \models_{v[a/x]} \varphi(x)$ for some $a \in \mathrm{Dom}_s$. Since $\mathcal{F}$ has expanding domains, $a \in \mathrm{Dom}_t$. Therefore, $\mathcal{M}, t \models_{v[a/x]} P\varphi(x)$ for some $a \in \mathrm{Dom}_t$, so $\mathcal{M}, t \models_v \exists x P \varphi(x)$. Thus, $\mathcal{M}, t \models_v P\exists x \varphi(x) \rightarrow \exists x P \varphi(x)$. The proof that $\mathcal{F} \models_{VD} CBF_G$ is very similar.

Now, suppose, for example, that $\mathcal{F} \models_{VD} BF_H$.

Take the particular case where $\varphi(x) = Q(x)$, for a unary predicate Q. Then, by the existential version of BF_H, we have $\mathcal{F} \models_{VD} P\exists x Q(x) \rightarrow \exists x PQ(x)$.

I will show that $\mathcal{F} = (T, <, \mathcal{D}, \mathrm{Dom})$ has expanding domains. Consider any $s, t \in T$ such that $s < t$ and let $a \in \mathrm{Dom}_s$. We want to show that $a \in \mathrm{Dom}_t$. Consider a model $\mathcal{M} = (T, <, \mathcal{D}, \mathrm{Dom}, \mathcal{I})$ on $\mathcal{F}$, where $I_s(Q) = \{a\}$ and $I_u(Q) = \emptyset$ for every $u \in T$ where $u \neq t$. Take an assignment v such that $v(x) = a$. Then $\mathcal{M}, s \models_{v[a/x]} Q(x)$ and $a \in \mathrm{Dom}_s$, so $\mathcal{M}, s \models_v \exists x Q(x)$. Therefore, $\mathcal{M}, t \models_v P\exists x Q(x)$. Then, by the existential version of BF_H, $\mathcal{M}, t \models_v \exists x PQ(x)$. Therefore, $\mathcal{M}, t \models_{v[b/x]} PQ(x)$ for some $b \in \mathrm{Dom}_t$, hence $\mathcal{M}, t' \models_{v[b/x]} Q(x)$ for some $t' < t$. This is only possible if $t' = s$ and $b = a$. Thus, $a \in \mathrm{Dom}_t$.

The proof in the case when $\mathcal{F} \models_{VD} CBF_G$ is analogous and left to the reader. The proofs of the equivalences in claim 2 are completely analogous, too.

Thus, the Future Barcan scheme BF_G semantically corresponds to the converse Past Barcan scheme CBF_H, and vice versa. These equivalences imply that an augmented temporal frame $\mathcal{F}$ has locally constant domains iff either of the following formulae is VD-valid in $\mathcal{F}$:

$\mathsf{BF_G} \wedge \mathsf{BF_H}$, $\mathsf{CBF_G} \wedge \mathsf{CBF_H}$, $\mathsf{BF_G} \wedge \mathsf{CBF_G}$, or $\mathsf{BF_H} \wedge \mathsf{CBF_H}$.

Now, let us look at some non-validities in the varying domain semantics.

1. It is not difficult to see that the Future Barcan formula scheme $\mathsf{BF_G}$ is, in general, not valid in models with expanding domains. Indeed, consider the special case where $\varphi(x) = Q(x)$, for a unary predicate Q. Then, the existential version of $\mathsf{BF_G}$ is $\mathsf{F}\exists x Q(x) \rightarrow \exists x \mathsf{F} Q(x)$.

   Now, consider the model $\mathcal{M} = (T, <, \mathcal{D}, \mathrm{Dom}, \mathcal{I})$, where $T = \{s,t\}$, $< = \{(s,s),(s,t),(t,t)\}$, $\mathcal{D} = \{a,b\}$, $\mathrm{Dom}_s = \{a\}$, $\mathrm{Dom}_t = \{a,b\}$, $I_s(Q) = \emptyset$, and $I_t(Q) = \{b\}$. $\mathcal{M}$ is a model with expanding domains.

   Take an assignment v such that $v(x) = b$. Then $\mathcal{M}, t \models_{v[b/x]} Q(x)$ and $b \in \mathrm{Dom}_t$, so $\mathcal{M}, t \models_v \exists x Q(x)$, therefore $\mathcal{M}, s \models_v \mathsf{F}\exists x Q(x)$.

   However, $\mathcal{M}, s \not\models_v \exists x \mathsf{F} Q(x)$. For, suppose otherwise. Since $\mathrm{Dom}_s = \{a\}$, then $\mathcal{M}, s \models_{v[a/x]} \mathsf{F} Q(x)$, hence $\mathcal{M}, s \models_{v[a/x]} Q(x)$ or $\mathcal{M}, t \models_{v[a/x]} Q(x)$, but neither of these holds.

2. Likewise, $\mathsf{CBF_H}$ is generally not valid in models with expanding domains.

3. Respectively $\mathsf{BF_H}$ and $\mathsf{BF_G}$ fail in some models with shrinking domains.

8.6.2 An Axiomatic System for Presentist Semantics

Here is an axiomatic system **FOTL(VD)** for the VD-validities.

I. *Axiom schemes:*

1. All axioms of the minimal propositional temporal logic $\mathbf{K}_t$.
2. Restricted Universal Instantiation ($\forall$-Elimination):
   $\forall y (\forall x \varphi(x) \rightarrow \varphi[y/x])$ for any y (free for substitution for x in φ).
3. Vacuous Generalisation: $\forall x \varphi \leftrightarrow \varphi$, if x does not occur free in φ.
4. $\forall$-Distributivity: $\forall x (\varphi \rightarrow \psi) \rightarrow (\forall x \varphi \rightarrow \forall x \psi)$.
5. $\forall$-Permutation: $\forall x \forall y \varphi \rightarrow \forall y \forall x \varphi$.
6. Reflexivity of equality: $\forall x (x = x)$.
7. Extensionality: $\forall x \forall y (x = y \rightarrow (\varphi[x/z] \rightarrow \varphi[y/z]))$.
8. Necessity of non-equality: $\forall x \forall y (x \neq y \rightarrow A(x \neq y))$.
   (Recall that $A\varphi$ stands for $\mathsf{H}\varphi \wedge \varphi \wedge \mathsf{G}\varphi$.)

II. *Inference rules* (where $\vdash_{\mathrm{VD}}$ denotes derivability in **FOTL(VD)**):

1. Modus Ponens: If $\vdash_{\mathrm{VD}} \varphi \rightarrow \psi$ and $\vdash_{\mathrm{VD}} \varphi$, then $\vdash_{\mathrm{VD}} \psi$.
2. G-Necessitation: If $\vdash_{\mathrm{VD}} \varphi$, then $\vdash_{\mathrm{VD}} \mathsf{G}\varphi$.
3. H-Necessitation: If $\vdash_{\mathrm{VD}} \varphi$, then $\vdash_{\mathrm{VD}} \mathsf{H}\varphi$.

Note that formulae like $\exists x G(x = \tau)$, $G \exists x(x = \tau)$ (where τ is a term), and $\forall y G \exists x G(x = y)$, that are derivable in the system **FOTL(CD)** are not valid in the presentist semantics and not derivable in **FOTL(VD)**.

8.7 The Existence Predicate

While presentism and eternalism are alternative theories in the philosophy of time, their respective technical manifestations are interreducible. On the one hand, constant domain semantics with eternalist quantification can be obtained from varying domain semantics with presentist quantification by imposing the condition that the Barcan Formula schemes and their converses are valid. On the other hand, varying domain semantics can be simulated in constant domain semantics by adding to the language of FOTL an **existence predicate** for *'existence at the current instant'*,[34] which can be defined in varying domain semantics by $E(\tau) := \exists z(z = \tau)$, but not in the constant domain semantics. With the existence predicate at our disposal, a sentence like *'Some philosopher exists who was a teacher of Alexander the Great'* can be formalised in two different ways:

(1) $\exists x(\text{philosopher}(x) \wedge P \text{ teacher-of-Alexander-the-Great}(x))$.
(2) $\exists x(E(x) \wedge \text{philosopher}(x) \wedge P \text{ teacher-of-Alexander-the-Great}(x))$.

While (1) is true at the present instant in the constant domain semantics with eternalist quantification, it is false at present in the varying domain semantcs. For the same reason, (2) is presently false in the constant domain semantics, but it was true in the year 340 BC. To generalise, for every formula φ of FOTL, its *E*-**relativisation** in the extended language can be obtained by replacing every occurrence of $\forall x$ in φ with '$\forall x(E(x) \rightarrow \ldots)$' and every occurrence of $\exists x$ with '$\exists x(E(x) \wedge \ldots)$'. Then the following holds:

For any FOTL *sentence φ not containing E, φ is true in a given model and possible world in it in the presentist semantics if and only if its E-relativisation $\rho(\varphi)$ is true there in the eternalist semantics.*

This can be proved by a routine structural induction on φ. The key inductive steps are for $\varphi = \forall x \psi$ and $\varphi = \exists x \psi$. It suffices to note that in each of them, given the inductive hypothesis, the truth conditions for $\forall x(E(x) \rightarrow \rho(\psi))$, respectively, $\exists x(E(x) \wedge \rho(\psi))$ are equivalent to the respective truth conditions for $\forall x \psi$ and $\exists x \psi$ in the presentist semantics. I leave the details to the reader.

One can abandon the classical rules for the quantifiers and adopt, instead, the rules for Free Logic, which is a version of first-order logic that allows for terms

---

[34] From a philosophical point of view, however, the question of whether existence is a legitimate predicate is debatable.

that do not refer to any existing entity. In Free Logic the application of the rule of Universal Instantiation is restricted by adding the predicate E for 'existence at the current instant', and Universal Generalisation is modified accordingly:

- *Universal Instantiation* ($\forall$-Elimination):
  $\vdash \forall x \varphi(x) \rightarrow (E(y) \rightarrow \varphi[y/x])$, where y is not free in φ.
- *Universal Generalisation* ($\forall$-Introduction):
  If $\vdash \psi \rightarrow (E(x) \rightarrow \varphi(x))$, then $\vdash \psi \rightarrow \forall x \varphi(x)$, where x is not free in ψ.

8.8 On Proper Names, Definite Descriptions, Rigid and Non-rigid Designations

Another essential issue arising in FOTL is about the interpretation of *individual terms*, referring to objects or individuals in the (local or global) domain which may change over time. Such references can be made in different ways.

A most common way of referring to individuals is by using **proper names** (formally represented by constant symbols in logical languages), such as 'the number 1', 'the number π', 'Bertrand Russell', 'Jorge Mario Bergoglio', 'Carl XVI Gustaf', and so on. These are always interpreted by the same object,[35] whether or not it actually exists at the present instant.

More generally, references to individuals are made by **definite descriptions**, usually expressed formally by functions, or by unary predicates (either primitive, or definable in the language) that are always interpreted as a singleton set of objects, thus designating the single object in that set in a definitive way: 'the least positive integer', 'the ratio between the circumference of a circle and its diameter', 'the junior author of *Principia Mathematica*', 'the present Pope', 'the current King of Sweden', and so on. Such definite descriptions define **individual concepts**. They may denote the same objects at all instants (more generally, in all possible worlds), and then they are called **rigid designators** (as is the case with the first three examples). Or, they may not denote the same objects at different instants (like the last two examples), and then they are **non-rigid designators**. Thus, proper names and definite descriptions referring to the same object at a given instant may have different semantic behaviour and are generally not inter-replaceable. For example '*The (current) King of Sweden is Carl XVI Gustaf*' is true at the time of writing this text, but it was not true in 1900 and most likely will not be true in 2100. Likewise, '*The Pope has been*

---

[35] Though the concept of 'sameness over time' is not unproblematic, cf. the Ship of Theseus. One formal way of handling identity across possible worlds is Lewis's "Counterpart theory", see e.g., Garson (1984)

the sovereign of the Vatican City since 1929' is true, whereas '*Pope Francis has been the sovereign of the Vatican City since 1929*' is false.

Note that if constants are treated as rigid designators, the principle of *Necessity of Identity* $\tau_1 = \tau_2 \rightarrow A(\tau_1 = \tau_2)$ is valid (recall that $A\varphi$ stands for $H\varphi \wedge \varphi \wedge G\varphi$), for both variables and constants. However, the language may also contain individual terms for which this principle fails. This typically happens with definite descriptions, such as 'the King of Sweden', or 'the Pope', which may refer to different objects at different times. Thus, proper names and definite descriptions require different semantic treatments and are not freely inter-substitutable.

More problematic are definite description terms like 'the present king of France' that may not (and, currently do not) describe any object, so the statement '*The present king of France does not exist*' is unquestionably true, but providing formal semantics to justify that truth is problematic. And, what about, for example, '*The king of France existed, but no longer exists.*'? Or, '*Le roi est mort, vive le roi!*'?

Assuming future non-determinism, definite descriptions need not refer to the same object even when used at the same instant but considered over alternative time histories. Thus, under the Ockhamist branching time semantics, statements about them made at a given instant may have different truth values depending on which possible future will be realised. For instance, '*The next president of the USA will be blond*' or '*the first child to be born in South Africa in 2050 will be a girl*' uttered now (at the time of writing this text) may refer to different people at alternative futures that are currently considered possible, and may be respectively true or false on these futures now. Furthermore, some definite descriptions that are temporally rigid may be modally non-rigid, or vice versa. Thus, those who accept future non-determinism would have to consider such descriptions as non-rigid designators in both temporal and alethic senses.

Now, in the formal semantics presented here, variable assignments are defined globally, and hence individual variables refer to the same object at all times. The interpretation of constant symbols, on the other hand, is specified locally, relative to an instant, even though the respective extensions range over the global domain. From a philosophical point of view, it seems natural to treat constant symbols as proper names or, more generally, as rigid designators, that is, to impose the additional requirement that their interpretations are constant across different times. Constant symbols can then be used to identify an object over time. For instance, treating a as a name for Aristotle, the sentence '*Aristotle existed but no longer exists*' can be formalised in the varying domain semantics as $P\exists x(x = a) \wedge \neg\exists x(x = a)$.

One way to deal with the problems around definite descriptions and what they denote is to switch from an extensional to an intensional account of individual terms. That is, rather than assigning to each term at each instant an *extension*, that is, an object from the domain, one may assign to each term an *intension*, that is, a function from instants to objects. A general framework in which individual terms are assigned both extensions and intensions is the *Case Intensional First-Order Logic* (CIFOL) proposed in Belnap and Müller (2014a) and Belnap and Müller (2014b). In CIFOL, identity is extensional, predication is intensional, and individuals can be identified across times without making use of rigid designation.

Lastly, a powerful and general syntactic mechanism for abstracting predicates from formulae and representing intentions is *predicate abstraction*. It is presented and explained in detail in Fitting and Fitting and Mendelsohn (1998), with many examples demonstrating its use for formal handling of most of the problems in first-order modal and temporal logics discussed here.

8.9 On Technical Results for First-Order Temporal Logics

First-order temporal logics are very expressive, and this often comes with a high computational price: these logics can be deductively very complex and are typically *highly* undecidable. For instance, the FOTL with constant domain semantics over the natural numbers, with only two variables and unary relation symbols, is already not only undecidable but not even recursively axiomatisable. Few axiomatisable, and even fewer decidable, natural fragments of FOTL have been identified so far. They include FOTL with *Since* and *Until* over the rationals, the fragment T(FOs) of FOTL, where temporal operators may not occur inside the scope of a quantifier, and the *monodic fragment*, only allowing formulae with at most one free variable in the scope of a temporal operator.

Some References

For further readings on first-order temporal logics, including philosophical aspects, semantics, deductive systems, (non)axiomatisabilty, (un)decidability, and other technical results, see Rescher and Urquhart (1971, chs. XIII and XX), McArthur (1976, ch. 4), Garson (1984), Merz (1992), Gabbay et al. (1994, ch. 14), Linsky and Zalta (1994), van Benthem (1995, section 7), Reynolds (1996), Fitting and Mendelsohn (1998), Wölfl (1999), Hodkinson, Wolter, and Zakharyaschev (2000), Hodkinson, Wolter, and Zakharyaschev (2001), Hodkinson, Wolter, and Zakharyaschev (2002), Wolter and Zakharyaschev (2002), Cocchiarella (2002), Kurucz et al. (2003), Lindström and Segerberg (2007), Kröger and Merz (2008), Dyke and Bardon (2013), Meyer (2013), Gallois (2016), Emery et al. (2020), Ludlow (2021), Fitting (2022).

9 Variations, Extensions, and Applications of Temporal Logics

There are many variations and extensions of temporal logics that have not been discussed so far. It is not possible to cover them properly in this short Element, so I will only give a selective and very brief overview of the more interesting and important species of other temporal logics.

9.1 Interval Temporal Logics

As already noted earlier, Prior's temporal operators are not well suited for capturing the distinctions between simple and progressive tenses, for example, as in '*I walked to the lake*' vs '*I was walking to the lake*'. Also, sentences like '*Bill was drinking his tea when the postman came*', or '*Bill always drinks his tea while reading the morning paper*' cannot be naturally captured in Prior's tense logic TL or in any of its extensions presented so far. For these, an alternative logical framework is needed, where the primary entities are *time intervals*, instead of instants, and temporal operators based on them feature in the logical language. That leads to the idea of *interval-based models and logics of time*.

Instant-based and interval-based models of time are based on different temporal ontologies. Though they are technically reducible to each other, the main semantic issue arising when designing logical formalisms to capture temporal reasoning remains: should propositions about time, and therefore formulae in the logical language, be interpreted as referring to instants or to intervals? Unlike the temporal logics presented so far, in interval-based temporal logics, formulae are evaluated relative to time intervals rather than instants.

Here I will briefly present the most popular propositional interval temporal logic, **Halpern and Shoham's interval logic**, hereafter denoted by HS , proposed in Halpern and Shoham (1991). The underlying idea is that each of Allen's binary relations between intervals, listed in the table in Figure 1 in Section 2.2, gives rise to a unary modal operator over relational structures where time intervals, rather than instants, are the primitive entities. Thus, HS is a multimodal logic, with formulae recursively defined by the following grammar:

$$\varphi := p \in \text{PROP} \mid \perp \mid \neg\varphi \mid (\varphi \wedge \varphi) \mid Z\varphi,$$

for $Z \in \{\langle L \rangle, \langle A \rangle, \langle O \rangle, \langle E \rangle, \langle D \rangle, \langle B \rangle, \langle \overline{L} \rangle, \langle \overline{A} \rangle, \langle \overline{O} \rangle, \langle \overline{E} \rangle, \langle \overline{D} \rangle, \langle \overline{B} \rangle \}$. These modal operators correspond to the binary interval relations Later, After,[36] Overlaps, Ends, During, Begins, displayed on Figure 1, and their inverses.

The standard semantics of the logic HS is based on instant-based models over linear time, where intervals are considered defined objects. Let $\mathcal{T} = \langle T, < \rangle$ be a temporal frame where the precedence relation $<$ is a strict linear order on the

---

[36] Also called 'meet', in Allen's paper and elsewhere (Allen 1983).

set of instants T. An **interval** in $\mathcal{T}$ is defined as an ordered pair $[a, b]$ such that $a, b \in T$ and $a \le b$. The set of all intervals in $\mathcal{T}$ is denoted by $\mathbb{I}(\mathcal{T})$. Note that the definition includes 'point intervals', of the type $[a, a]$. An **interval model** is a triple $\mathcal{M} = \langle T, \prec, V \rangle$ consisting of a temporal frame $\mathcal{T} = \langle T, \prec \rangle$ and a valuation V that assigns to each atomic proposition $p \in \text{PROP}$ a set of intervals $V(p) \subseteq \mathcal{P}(\mathbb{I}(\mathcal{T}))$ at which p is considered true. The **truth of a formula φ on a given interval $[a, b]$ in an interval model $\mathcal{M}$** is defined by structural induction on formulae, with the standard clauses for the propositional connectives, plus the following generic clause for the modal operators, which are given standard Kripke-style semantics over the associated Allen's relations:

$\mathcal{M}, [a, b] \models \langle X \rangle \varphi$ iff $\mathcal{M}, [c, d] \models \varphi$ for some interval $[c, d]$ such that $[a, b]\ R_X\ [c, d]$, where R_X is the interval relation corresponding to $\langle X \rangle$.

For each diamond modality $\langle X \rangle$, the corresponding box modality is defined as its dual: $[X]\varphi \equiv \neg \langle X \rangle \neg \varphi$. Sometimes, point-intervals are excluded and then the semantics is called **strict semantics**. The strict and non-strict semantics differ essentially in their respective validities. Here are some of the specific clauses in the strict semantics, followed by illustrations for all cases:

- The semantic clause for the operator associated with the relation 'After':

$$\mathcal{M}, [a, b] \models \langle A \rangle \varphi \text{ iff } \mathcal{M}, [b, c] \models \varphi \text{ for some } c > b.$$

- The clause for the operator associated with 'Before' (converse of After) is:

$$\mathcal{M}, [a, b] \models \langle \overline{A} \rangle \varphi \text{ iff } \mathcal{M}, [c, a] \models \varphi \text{ for some } c < a.$$

- The clause for the operator associated with 'Overlap' is:

$$\mathcal{M}, [a, b] \models \langle O \rangle \varphi \text{ iff } \mathcal{M}, [c, d] \models \varphi \text{ for some } c, d \text{ such that } a < c < b < d.$$

Here is a graphical representation of the modal operators in HS :

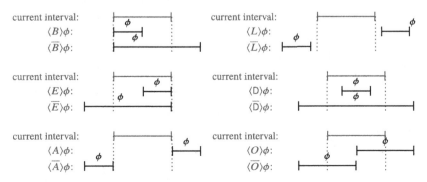

Some of the modalities in HS are definable in terms of others. Here are some expressively complete sets of operators in both versions of the semantics, with the respective defining equivalences for the remaining operators:

(i) In the strict semantics the six operators $\langle A \rangle$, $\langle B \rangle$, $\langle E \rangle$, $\langle \overline{A} \rangle$, $\langle \overline{B} \rangle$, $\langle \overline{E} \rangle$ suffice to express all others, as shown by the following equivalences:

$$\langle L \rangle \varphi \equiv \langle A \rangle \langle A \rangle \varphi, \qquad\qquad \langle \overline{L} \rangle \varphi \equiv \langle \overline{A} \rangle \langle \overline{A} \rangle \varphi,$$
$$\langle D \rangle \varphi \equiv \langle B \rangle \langle E \rangle \varphi, \qquad\qquad \langle \overline{D} \rangle \varphi \equiv \langle \overline{B} \rangle \langle \overline{E} \rangle \varphi,$$
$$\langle O \rangle \varphi \equiv \langle E \rangle \langle \overline{B} \rangle \varphi, \qquad\qquad \langle \overline{O} \rangle \varphi \equiv \langle B \rangle \langle \overline{E} \rangle \varphi.$$

(ii) In the non-strict semantics, the four operators $\langle B \rangle$, $\langle E \rangle$, $\langle \overline{B} \rangle$, $\langle \overline{E} \rangle$ suffice to express all others, as shown by the following equivalences:

$$\langle A \rangle \varphi \equiv ([E]\bot \wedge (\varphi \vee \langle \overline{B} \rangle \varphi)) \vee \langle E \rangle ([E]\bot \wedge (\varphi \vee \langle \overline{B} \rangle \varphi)),$$
$$\langle \overline{A} \rangle \varphi \equiv ([B]\bot \wedge (\varphi \vee \langle \overline{E} \rangle \varphi)) \vee \langle B \rangle ([B]\bot \wedge (\varphi \vee \langle \overline{E} \rangle \varphi)),$$
$$\langle L \rangle \varphi \equiv \langle A \rangle (\langle \overline{E} \rangle \top \wedge \langle A \rangle \varphi), \quad \langle \overline{L} \rangle \varphi \equiv \langle \overline{A} \rangle (\langle \overline{B} \rangle \top \wedge \langle \overline{A} \rangle \varphi),$$
$$\langle D \rangle \varphi \equiv \langle B \rangle \langle E \rangle \varphi, \quad \langle \overline{D} \rangle \varphi \equiv \langle \overline{B} \rangle \langle \overline{E} \rangle \varphi,$$
$$\langle O \rangle \varphi \equiv \langle E \rangle (\langle \overline{E} \rangle \top \wedge \langle \overline{B} \rangle \varphi), \quad \langle \overline{O} \rangle \varphi \equiv \langle B \rangle (\langle \overline{B} \rangle \top \wedge \langle \overline{E} \rangle \varphi).$$

The logic HS has over 1,000 expressively non-equivalent fragments involving only some of these modal operators. Halpern and Shoham's internal logic and most of its fragments are very expressive and the respective validities are usually undecidable (under some additional assumptions, even highly undecidable). However, some non-trivial decidable fragments of HS have been identified. The best-studied one is the *neighbourhood interval logic*, which involves the operators $\langle A \rangle$ and $\langle \overline{A} \rangle$.

There is a natural spatial interpretation of interval temporal logics, based on the idea that the pairs of points that define an interval on a linear order L can be considered coordinates of a point in the $L \times L$-plane, and the relations between intervals mapped to natural spatial relations between the corresponding points. For the case where $L = \mathbb{N}$, these correspondences are illustrated in Figure 5.

This interpretation has been used to transfer various technical results between spatial and interval logics, such as undecidability, by reduction from the tiling problem for (the 2nd octant of) $\mathbb{N} \times \mathbb{N}$.

The family of fragments and subsystems of HS has been extensively studied with respect to expressiveness and (un)decidability of satisfiability and model checking, but only a few complete axiomatic systems for them have been constructed so far, mostly for systems of neighbourhood interval logic on some classes of interval structures. One more notable axiom for $\langle A \rangle$ is the

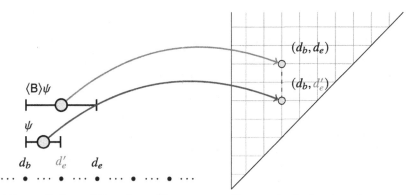

Figure 5 Every interval on $\mathbb{N}$ is represented by a point in the second octant. The spatial counterpart of the interval relation *Begins* is shown.

weak transitivity $\langle A \rangle \langle A \rangle \langle A \rangle p \rightarrow \langle A \rangle \langle A \rangle p$, essentially saying that any two consecutive right-neighbouring intervals can be joined into one right-neighbouring interval.

9.2 Hybrid, Metric, and Real-Time Temporal Logics

Hybrid temporal logics enrich the traditional propositional framework of TL and extensions by adding features of first-order logic, thus bringing the semantics into the language and thereby considerably increasing its expressive power. Historically, the idea behind hybrid logic was first conceived by Prior in order to solve a problem in the philosophy of time related to McTaggart's argument of unreality of time. The most essential feature in hybrid temporal logics are **nominals**, going back to Prior's 'clock variables'. These are special atomic propositions that are considered to be true at *exactly one instant* of the temporal model, so one can think of a nominal i as saying 'It is i o'clock now'. In addition to nominals, hybrid languages are often augmented by other suitable syntactic mechanisms, which I will briefly present here.

- **Satisfaction operator** @. This operator is used to express within the language the truth of a given formula at the instant in the model denoted by the nominal i. More precisely, $\mathcal{M}, t \vDash @_i \varphi$ holds just in case $\mathcal{M}, V(i) \vDash \varphi$, where $V(i)$ is the unique instant where i is true. Thus, the notion of truth at an instant of a temporal model is imported into the object-language.
- **Quantifiers over nominals.** By means of quantifying over nominals one can express that a given formula is true at a given instant in a temporal model under each possible assignment of instants to i. Formally, we define $\mathcal{M}, t \vDash \forall i \varphi$ iff $\mathcal{M}_{[i \rightarrow s]}, t \vDash \varphi$ for every instant s in $\mathcal{M}$, where $\mathcal{M}_{[i \rightarrow s]}$ is the model obtained from $\mathcal{M}$ by re-assigning the denotation of i to be s.

Thus, the power of first-order quantification is brought into the propositional object-language, while many of its propositional virtues are still preserved.

- **Reference pointers** (aka **binders**). The reference pointer $\downarrow_i$ binds the value of the nominal i to the current instant of evaluation. Thus, a formula $\downarrow_i \varphi$ is true at a given instant t in a temporal model iff φ is true at t whenever the nominal i denotes t. Formally, $\mathcal{M}, t \vDash \downarrow_i \varphi$ iff $\mathcal{M}_{[i \to t]}, t \vDash \varphi$. Reference pointers thus provide a mechanism for referring to the current instant, that is, saying 'now' and later (in the evaluation of the formula) 'then'.

Other operators that can be considered hybrid temporal logic operators are the **universal modality**, the **difference modality**, and **propositional quantifiers**. The universal modality A says that a given formula is true at every instant of the model and thus captures the *global* notion of truth in a model: $\mathcal{M}, t \vDash A\varphi$ iff $\mathcal{M} \vDash \varphi$. The difference modality D states that the given formula is true at some *other* instant. Thus, both modalities transcend the underlying accessibility relation. Propositional quantifiers $\forall p$ introduce (second-order) quantification over propositional variables into the propositional language.

Hybrid logic can be seen as capturing Prior's idea of 'third' and 'fourth' grades of 'temporal involvement', see (Øhrstrøm & Hasle, 1995, ch. 2.9).

Hybrid languages are quite expressive. Here are just two examples:

- Irreflexivity of the precedence, while not expressible in TL, can be expressed in a language with nominals and satisfaction operator $@_i$ as $@_i G\neg i$.
- The operators *Since* (S) and *Until* (U) are definable by using nominals and reference pointers: $\varphi U \psi := \downarrow_i F(\psi \land H(Pi \to \varphi))$ and likewise for S.

Various complete axiomatic systems of hybrid logics, for both linear and branching time logics, have been constructed. While the validities in weaker versions of hybrid logics – only with nominals, satisfaction operators, universal modality, and difference modality – are still decidable, the more expressive ones, with reference pointers or quantifiers over nominals, are usually undecidable.

Tableau-based methods and other classical deductive systems, like natural deduction and sequent calculi, have also been extensively developed for hybrid logics. Proof theory of hybrid logics has some clear advantages over the proof theory of ordinary modal and temporal logic, as shown in Braüner (2011).

Hybrid extensions have also proved to be useful for interval temporal logics. In fact, some hybrid operators (e.g., nominals, or difference and satisfaction operators) are definable in HS but not in various fragments and modifications of HS, which have been recently hybridised and studied, inter alia, in terms of expressive power and computational complexity, see Wałęga (2019).

Metric temporal logics go back to Prior, too. He used the notation $Pn\varphi$ for 'φ *was the case n time units ago*' and $Fn\varphi$ for 'φ *will be the case n time units from now*' (recall the formalisation of Lavenham's argument in Section 5.2). These operators presuppose that time can be measured by temporal units, which may be associated with clocks or calendars (e.g., hours, days, years, etc.). If the relevant units are days, for example, the operator F1 reads 'tomorrow', whereas F0 refers to 'now'. Prior also noted that $Pn\varphi$ can be defined as $F(-n)\varphi$ and the metric operators satisfy some basic principles, such as $FnFm\varphi \rightarrow F(n+m)\varphi$. The standard, non-metric versions of the temporal operators are definable in terms of the metric ones by using the following equivalences:

$$P\varphi \equiv \exists n(n < 0 \wedge Fn\varphi) \quad F\varphi \equiv \exists n(n > 0 \wedge Fn\varphi)$$
$$H\varphi \equiv \forall n(n < 0 \rightarrow Fn\varphi) \quad G\varphi \equiv \forall n(n > 0 \rightarrow Fn\varphi).$$

Various metric extensions of temporal logics on the real line as a model of time have been proposed as well, giving rise to **real-time logics**. These logics employ additional operators, illustrated in the sample sentence '*whenever p holds in the future, q will hold within 3 time units later*', such as:

- **time-bounded operators**: $G(p \rightarrow F_{\leq 3}q)$;
- **freeze quantifiers** (similar to the hybrid logic reference pointers): $Gx.(p \rightarrow Fy.(q \wedge y \leq x + 3))$;
- **quantifiers over time variables**: $\forall xG(p \wedge t = x \rightarrow F(q \wedge t \leq x + 3))$.

Amongst the most important metric and real-time temporal logics is the **metric temporal logic** (MTL), extending LTL by constraining the temporal operators by intervals on the real numbers. It was proposed in Koymans (1990) as a specification formalism for safety-critical real-time systems. Such metric and real-time extensions are usually very expressive and often lead to logics with undecidable decision problems. A way to regain decidability (e.g., for MTL) is to relax 'punctuality' requirements involving precise time durations, by replacing them with requirements involving time intervals.

Metric extensions have also been explored in interval temporal logics, see Bresolin et al. (2013).

9.3 Combining Temporal and Other Logics

Logic can be used to reason about dynamically changing aspects of the world, and time plays a crucial role in most other areas of human activity. For example, the notion of knowledge studied in *epistemic logics*, the physical concept of space in *spatial logics*, and the reasoning about ontologies in *description logics*, are all essentially related to time. It is therefore very natural to add a temporal

Philosophy and Logic

dimension to these logics and equip their respective languages with suitable temporal operators. Technically, there are several ways of combining models and logical systems: products, fusions, and so on. These constructions provide different mechanisms for temporalising a logic and raise generic questions about transfer of logical properties, such as axiomatisations, completeness, and decidability. Decidability, for instance, is usually preserved in fusions, while it is often lost in products of logical systems. Here I only mention and briefly discuss some of the most common cases of *temporalised logical systems*.

Temporal logics of agency. Temporal reasoning is a very important aspect of reasoning about agents and their attitudes, abilities, and actions. Various temporal logics of agency have been introduced and studied since the 1980s. One of the earliest, and probably most influential, philosophical studies of logics of agency is on the *Seeing to it that* (STIT) theories and logics, originated by Belnap and Perloff (1988). These logics contain formulae of the form 'stit φ', reading '*The agent sees to it that φ holds*', which allow one to reason about what agents can achieve by making suitable choices over time histories. Although the original versions of the STIT logics do not involve temporal operators, their semantics is based on Ockhamist branching time models, where an agent's choices at a given instant are represented by sets of histories passing through that instant (the possible futures where the respective choices are enforced), forming a partition of the set of all histories passing through that instant. Like in Ockhamist branching time logics, formulae in STIT are evaluated on pairs (history, instant). Intuitively, the formula stit φ is true at a given instant t with respect to a given history h iff the agent's choice at t with respect to h guarantees that φ, that is, if φ is true at t relative to all histories in the choice cluster.

Another important family of temporal logics of agency are the *alternating-time logic* ATL and its extension ATL*, introduced in Alur, Henzinger, and Kupferman (2002). These are multi-agent extensions of the computation tree logics CTL and CTL* (which can be regarded as the single-agent versions) and have become a standard logical framework for strategic reasoning in multi-agent systems. These logics extend the usual repertoire of temporal operators, for example in CTL, with *strategic path quantifiers* $\langle\langle C \rangle\rangle$, indexed with sets ('coalitions') C of agents. The formula $\langle\langle C \rangle\rangle \varphi$ intuitively says '*The coalition C has a collective strategy to guarantee that the goal φ is satisfied on every path enabled by that collective strategy*', where the goal φ is a temporalised formula. While STIT logics refer to an abstract notion of a history, ATL and ATL* are interpreted in *concurrent game structures*, in which histories are sequences of successor states generated by discrete transitions, just as in standard transition systems, but where the transitions are caused by collective actions of all agents.

Temporal-epistemic logics. These form a special family of temporal logics of agency, which bring together temporal logics and (multi-agent) logics of knowledge. Some important properties can naturally be expressed by combining the epistemic modality K ('the agent knows that') with temporal operators, for example *perfect recall*: $K\varphi \rightarrow GK\varphi$ ('*If the agent knows φ now, then the agent will always know φ in the future*') and *no learning*: $FK\varphi \rightarrow K\varphi$ ('*If the agent will know φ in the future, then the agent already knows φ now*'). Various temporal-epistemic logics were studied during the 1980s, mostly from the perspective of distributed computing and multiprocess systems. The comprehensive study by Halpern and Vardi (1989) considers a variety of ninety-six temporal-epistemic logics on so-called *interpreted systems*, consisting of sets of 'runs' in a transition system in which several agents act (or, processes run) in parallel, with partial observability on the state space for each agent. That variety is based on several parameters: *number of agents* (one or many), *the language* (with or without common knowledge), *the formal model of time* (linear or branching time), *recall abilities* (no recall, bounded recall, or perfect recall), *learning abilities* (learning or no learning), *synchrony* (synchronous or asynchronous), *unique initial state*. Depending on the particular choice of these parameters, the computational complexity of the decision problem for these logics ranges very broadly from PSPACE-complete to highly undecidable (Π_1^1-complete).

Spatial-temporal logics. Space and time are intimately related in the modern physical world, and they have become inseparable in modern physical theories, such as Einstein's relativity theory, based on Minkowski's four-dimensional space-time manifold. Spatial-temporal logics combine spatial and temporal reasoning in a unifying logical framework. Besides modern physics and cosmology, space-time reasoning and logics for it have been extensively explored in Artificial Intelligence (AI), particularly in the context of spatio-temporal databases, ontologies, and constraint networks. The main focus is on the logical characterisation of spatio-temporal models, expressiveness, and computational complexity. Two sustained research projects on space-time theories, with applications to relativity theory and quantum mechanics, are the *Branching Space-Times* theory (BST), originally developed in Belnap (1992) and more recently in the monograph Belnap et al. (2022), and the logic for relativity theory presented in Andréka, Madarász, and Németi (2007).

Temporal reasoning can naturally be combined with various other non-classical logical systems. Important cases include: temporal extensions of *description logics*, which involve *concepts* (unary predicates) and *roles* (binary predicates), used to describe and reason about various ontologies (biological, medical, geographic, etc.) and relations between the concepts in them;

two-dimensional temporal logics, especially in the context of temporal databases and other applications to AI, see Section 9.5.2; as well as *intuitionistic, deontic, many-valued, probabilistic, paraconsistent*, and other temporal logics.

9.4 On Logical Deduction and Decision Methods for Temporal Logics

Extensive research and numerous publications over the past fifty years have developed a variety of logical deduction systems and decision methods for the temporal logics mentioned here and many more. *Hilbert-style axiomatic systems* are the most common logical deduction systems for temporal logics, but many complete systems of *semantic tableaux, sequent calculi*, and *resolution-based systems* have been constructed as well. One of the most important logical decision problems is to determine whether a given formula of a given logic is satisfiable (respectively, valid) in the semantics provided for that logic. Particularly efficient and practically useful for deciding satisfiability and (non-)validity are the *tableaux-based methods*, originating from the pioneering works of Beth, Hintikka, Smullyan, and Fitting. These methods are based on a systematic search for a satisfying model (respectively, falsifying counter-model) of an input formula that is tested for satisfiability (respectively, validity, that is, non-falsifiability), and they are guaranteed to find such a model whenever it exists. Other methods that have proven practically very useful for deciding satisfiability as well as for model checking of temporal logics in computer science are the *automata-based methods*, which have been actively developing since the early 1990s. These methods transform temporal formulae into *automata on infinite words* (for linear-time logics) or *on infinite trees* (for branching-time logics) and represent models for the logics as input objects (respectively, infinite words or trees) for their associated automata. Thus, satisfiability of a formula becomes equivalent to non-emptiness of the language of the associated automaton. These methods are based on classical results about decidability of the monadic second-order theories of the order of natural numbers (*Büchi's theorem*) and of the infinite binary tree (*Rabin's theorem*). Automata on infinite words and Büchi's theorem were used to obtain decision procedures for LTL, whereas automata on infinite trees and Rabin's theorem were used to obtain decision procedures for CTL*.

While most propositional temporal logics are decidable, adding some syntactic or semantic features can make them explode computationally and become undecidable. The most common causes of undecidability of temporal logics, besides combinations with other expressive logics, include: grid-like models; products of temporal logics; interval-based logics with no locality assumptions;

time-reference mechanisms, such as reference pointers and freeze quantifiers; exact time constraints, and so on. There are various ways to tame temporal logics and restore decidability, such as adding syntactic and parametric restrictions (e.g., on the number of propositional variables or the depth of nesting), imposing suitable semantic restrictions (e.g., locality for interval logics), identifying decidable fragments (e.g., the two-variable fragment FO^2 of classical first-order logic, guarded fragments, monodic fragments), among others.

9.5 On Applications of Temporal Logics

The initial development of temporal logics was driven by philosophical motivations. Over the years, many temporal logical formalisms emerged with various other motivations, coming from computer science, AI, linguistics, natural, cognitive, and social sciences. Here I only mention some applications of temporal logics, with a few key references for each.

9.5.1 Temporal Logics in Computer Science

The idea of applying temporal reasoning to the analysis of deterministic and stochastic transition systems was already present in the theory of processes and events in Rescher and Urquhart (1971, ch. XIV). However, temporal logic became really prominent in computer science in the mid-1970s with the seminal paper Pnueli (1977) and a few precursors. Pnueli proposed application of temporal logics to the specification and verification of *reactive and concurrent programs and systems*. In order to ensure correct behaviour of a reactive program, in which computations are non-terminating (e.g., an operating system), it is necessary to formally specify and verify the acceptable infinite executions of that program. Key properties of infinite computations in transition systems that can be captured by temporal expressions include *liveness, safety, and fairness*.

- **Liveness** properties, or **eventualities**, involve temporal patterns of forms like Fp, $q \rightarrow Fp$, or $G(q \rightarrow Fp)$, which ensure that if a specific precondition (q) is initially satisfied, then a desirable state (satisfying p) will eventually be reached in the course of the computation. Some examples: '*If a message is sent, it will eventually be delivered*' and '*Whenever a printing job is started, it will eventually be completed*'.

- **Safety** or **invariance** properties involve temporal patterns of forms like Gp, $q \rightarrow Gp$, or $G(q \rightarrow Gp)$, which ensure that if a specific precondition (q) is initially satisfied, then undesirable states (violating the safety condition p) will never occur. Some examples: '*No more than one process will be in its critical section at any moment of time*', '*A resource will never be used by two* *or more processes simultaneously'*, '*The traffic lights will never show green in all directions*', '*A train will never pass a red semaphore*'.

- **Fairness** properties involve combinations of temporal patterns of the forms GFp ('*infinitely often p*') or FGp ('*eventually always p*'). Intuitively, fairness requires that whenever several resource-sharing processes are run concurrently, they must be treated 'fairly' by the operating system, scheduler, or similar. A typical fairness requirement says that if a process is persistent in sending a request (keeps sending it over and over again), its request will eventually be granted.

As shown in Sections 4.4, 6.4, and 7.5, these can be naturally formalised in the logics LTL, CTL, and CTL*. Then, algorithms and computational tools designed for these logics can be used for formal verification and model synthesis. For more see Manna and Pnueli (1992) and other references at the end of the section.

Another important idea for applications of temporal logics in computer science, presented and promoted in Gabbay (1987), is that of *executable temporal logic*, based on the concept of *declarative past vs imperative future* and indicating that temporal logic can serve as a unifying background for the declarative and imperative paradigms in programming.

9.5.2 Temporal Logics in Artificial Intelligence

Artificial Intelligence (AI) is one of the major areas of application of temporal logics. Relating temporal reasoning to AI was suggested already in the early philosophical discussion on AI by McCarthy and Hayes (1969) and in the theory of processes and events in Rescher and Urquhart (1971, ch. XIV). See Øhrstrøm and Hasle (1995) for an overview of these early developments. In the 1980s, temporal representation and reasoning gradually became an increasingly prominent theme in AI with several influential works, including work on temporal logic for reasoning about processes and plans in McDermott (1982), a general theory of action and time in Allen (1984), the Event Calculus by Kowalski and Sergot (1986), the system of temporal database management by Dean and McDermott (1987), and others. Influential works in the 1990s include the introduction of interval-based temporal logics by Halpern and Shoham (1991) and by Allen and Ferguson (1994) with representation of actions and events, the Situation Calculus of Pinto and Reiter (1995), the Action Theory of Lamport (1994), and so on. Further important developments relating temporal reasoning and AI since then include: temporal reasoning in natural language, temporal ontologies, temporal databases and constraint solving, temporal planning, executable temporal logics, spatial-temporal reasoning, temporal reasoning in agent-based systems, and others. The field has gradually grown very broad and rich, as witnessed by the twenty-chapter handbook Fisher et al. (2005).

9.5.3 Temporal Logics in Natural Language Semantics and Linguistics

Time and tense are very important aspects of natural languages, and they have naturally been a major source of inspiration for developments in temporal logics, way before their applications to computer science and AI emerged, at least as early as the seminal work by Reichenbach (1947). Reichenbach provided a systematic semantic analysis of tenses in natural language, according to which each tense is characterised by the temporal relationships amongst a triple of time points related to its use, namely: *event time* (E), *reference time* (R), and *speech time* (S). Using these, he classified most of the natural tenses, for example, *present*, where they all coincide, *present perfect*, where E precedes S and R which coincide, *past perfect*, where E precedes R, which precedes S, and so on. Prior's invention of tense logic was also strongly motivated by the use of tenses in natural language. Reichenbach's analysis cannot account for the full spectrum of tenses used in natural language, most notably not for progressive tenses, which are more naturally captured by interval-based logics, as pointed out in Section 9.1. Subsequently, that analysis was refined and extended to capture not only tenses but also other natural-language temporal expressions, such as temporal prepositions and binary relations between instants or intervals 'before', 'after', 'since', 'during', until). Several temporal logics have been successfully used for that purpose.

An important crossing point of natural language and temporal logics is the theory of *counterfactual conditionals*, where temporal reasoning plays a crucial role and branching time models and logics become naturally applicable. Just one (real life) example: '*If I had not committed two months ago to completing this book by the end of this month, I would now be enjoying my summer holidays on the beach instead of working round the clock on this job.*'

Yet another influential development on the border of logic and natural language, with a strong temporal flavour, is the Discourse Representation Theory, systematically presented in Kamp and Reyle (1993), where a dynamic view on the semantics of natural language is developed.

Some References

For further readings on interval-based temporal logics, see Hamblin (1972), Humberstone (1979), Röper (1980), Burgess (1982a), Moszkowski (1983), Allen (1984), Halpern and Shoham (1991), Venema (1990), Venema (1991),

Hansen and Chaochen (1997), Marx and Reynolds (1999), Goranko, Montanari, and Sciavicco (2003), and the surveys Goranko, Montanari, and Sciavicco (2004) and Della Monica et al. (2011).

For readings on hybrid logics, see Prior (1967, ch. 5), Prior (1968, ch. 11), Bull (1970), Kamp (1971), Alur and Henzinger (1994), Goranko (1996), Areces and ten Cate (2006), Blackburn (2006), Braüner (2022).

On metric and real-time temporal logics see Prior (1967, ch. 6), Rescher and Urquhart (1971, ch. X), Koymans (1990), Alur and Henzinger (1992), Alur and Henzinger (1993), Montanari (1996), Montanari and Policriti (1996), Reynolds (2010), Bresolin et al. (2013), Reynolds (2014).

On other variations and extensions of temporal logics see Rescher and Urquhart (1971, chs. XVIII and XIX), Finger and Gabbay (1992), Finger and Gabbay (1996), Alur et al. (2002), Finger et al. (2002), Kesten and Pnueli (2002), Kurucz et al. (2003), Reynolds and French (2003), Goranko and van Drimmelen (2006), Demri et al. (2016). For temporal extensions of STIT logics see Broersen (2011) and Lorini (2013).

On combinations of temporal with epistemic, spatial, agentive, and other logics, see Rescher and Urquhart (1971, ch. XVI), Halpern and Vardi (1989), Belnap (1992), Artale and Franconi (2000), Wolter and Zakharyaschev (2000), Fagin et al. (1995), Gabelaia et al. (2005), van Benthem and Pacuit (2006), Uckelman and Uckelman (2007), Andréka et al. (2007), Kontchakov et al. (2007), Lutz, Wolter, and Zakharyaschev (2008), Müller (2014), Carnielli and Coniglio (2020), Belnap et al. (2022).

General references on deductive systems for temporal logics include: Rescher and Urquhart (1971), McArthur (1976), Burgess (1984), Emerson (1990), Goldblatt (1992), Gabbay et al. (1994), Bolc and Szałas (1995), van Benthem (1995), Fitting and Mendelsohn (1998), Gabbay and Guenthner (2002), Kurucz et al. (2003), Fisher et al. (2005), Kröger and Merz (2008), Fisher (2011), Demri et al. (2016).

On decidability results and decision procedures using tableaux-based and automata-based methods for various temporal logics see Burgess (1980), Ben-Ari et al. (1983), Emerson and Sistla (1984), Emerson and Halpern (1985), Burgess and Gurevich (1985), Gurevich and Shelah (1985), Wolper (1985), Goldblatt (1992), Goré (1999), Kontchakov et al. (2004), Reynolds (2007), Vardi (2007), Baier and Katoen (2008), Goranko and Shkatov (2010), Reynolds (2011), Reynolds (2014), Demri et al. (2016).

On temporal logics in AI and computer science see also Kowalski and Sergot (1986), Galton (1987), Emerson (1990), Manna and Pnueli (1992), Vila (1994), Bolc and Szałas (1995), Galton (1995), Gabbay, Reynolds, and Finger (2000),

Pani and Bhattacharjee (2001), Baier and Katoen (2008), Fisher (2008), Kröger and Merz (2008), Fisher (2011), Demri et al. (2016).

On applications of temporal logics in natural language and linguistics, see Steedman (1997), ter Meulen (2005), Hamm and Bott (2021).

9.6 Finally, on What Is Not in the Element

Due to space limitations, many important topics of temporal logics have only been briefly mentioned or have even been completely left out of the Element, so let me at least mention what the Element is lacking and the reader may wish to research further.

Of the conceptual and philosophical aspects of temporal logics, I have essentially not discussed the interactions of time with alethic modalities (cf. Prior (1957); Thomason (1984); Wölfl (1999); Cocchiarella (2002)), with tense (cf. Kuhn and Portner (2002)), or with physical space (cf. Belnap et al. (2022)).

On the technical side, I have not even mentioned model theory of temporal logics, nor have I presented any completeness, decidability, or undecidability proofs, (non-)expressiveness or complexity results, nor tableaux or any other deductive systems, except axiomatic ones. For good overviews of these missing topics, from the many references listed earlier in the section, I select the handbook chapters Burgess (2002), van Benthem (1995), Goré (1999), and Finger et al. (2002).

Epilogue: Past, Present, and Future of Temporal Logics

As demonstrated in this Element temporal logics have had diverse and expanding motivations and areas of application throughout their history, starting from philosophy and theology in the distant past, and gradually also coming to encompass linguistics, computer science, AI, physics and other natural sciences, and more, in the present. Where, then, does the future of temporal logics lie? Predicting the future is a risky endeavour, but still, let me share my conviction that temporal logics will continue to broaden and deepen in relevance and scope, while also integrating various hitherto-unrelated developments in temporal and other logics into increasingly complex and powerful logical systems, combining temporality with numerous other facets of human activity and reasoning. A key line of future developments of temporal logics will focus on temporal aspects of agency and multi-agent systems, including knowledge, beliefs, learning, actions, abilities, normative and strategic reasoning, and so on. For more, we await the future.

References

Allen, J. (1983). Maintaining knowledge about Temporal Intervals. *Communications of the ACM*, *26*(11), 832–43.

Allen, J. (1984). Towards a general theory of action and time. *Artificial Intelligence*, *23*(2), 123–54.

Allen, J., & Ferguson, G. (1994). Actions and events in interval temporal logic. *Journal of Logic and Computation*, *4*(5), 531–79.

Alur, R., & Henzinger, T. A. (1992). Logics and models of real time: A survey. In J. W. de Bakker, C. Huizing, W. P. de Roever, & G. Rozenberg (Eds.), *Real-time: Theory in practice* (pp. 74–106). Springer.

Alur, R., & Henzinger, T. (1993). Real-time logics: Complexity and expressiveness. *Information and Computation*, *104*(1), 35–77.

Alur, R., & Henzinger, T. A. (1994). A really temporal logic. *Journal of the ACM*, *41*(1), 181–203.

Alur, R., Henzinger, T. A., & Kupferman, O. (2002). Alternating-time temporal logic. *Journal of the ACM*, *49*(5), 672–713.

Andréka, H., Madarász, J. X., & Németi, I. (2007). Logic of space-time and relativity theory. In M. Aiello, I. Pratt-Hartmann, & J. Van Benthem (Eds.), *Handbook of Spatial Logics* (pp. 607–711). Springer.

Areces, C., & ten Cate, B. (2006). Hybrid logics. In *Handbook of modal logic*. Elsevier.

Aristotle. (1984/350 BC). *Organon II. On Interpretation*. In *Complete Works of Aristotle*, ed. Jonathan Barnes. Princeton University Press.

Artale, A., & Franconi, E. (2000). A survey of temporal extensions of description logics. *Annals of Mathematics and Artificial Intelligence*, *30*, 171–210.

Baier, C., & Katoen, J.-P. (2008). *Principles of model checking*. MIT Press.

Barcan, R. C. (1946). A functional calculus of first order based on strict implication. *The Journal of Symbolic Logic*, *11*(1), 1–16.

Belnap, N. (1992). Branching space-time. *Synthese*, *92*(3), 385–434.

Belnap, N., & Green, M. (1994). Indeterminism and the Thin Red Line. *Philosophical Perspectives*, *8*, 365–88.

Belnap, N., & Müller, T. (2014a). CIFOL: Case-intensional first order logic. *Journal of Philosophical Logic* (I) Toward a Theory of Sorts., *43*(2–3), 393–437.

Belnap, N., & Müller, T. (2014b). BH-CIFOL: Case-intensional first order logic. *Journal of Philosophical Logic* (II) Branching Histories., *43*(5), 835–66.

Belnap, N., Müller, T., & Placek, T. (2022). *Branching space-times. Theory and applications*. Oxford University Press.

Belnap, N., & Perloff, M. (1988). Seeing to it that: A canonical form for agentives. *Theoria, 54*, 175–99.

Belnap, N., Perloff, M., & Xu, M. (2001). *Facing the future: Agents and choices in our indeterminist world*. Oxford University Press.

Ben-Ari, M., Pnueli, A., & Manna, Z. (1983). The temporal logic of branching time. *Acta Informatica, 20*, 207–26.

Blackburn, P. (2006). Arthur Prior and hybrid logic. *Synthese, 150*(3), 329–72.

Blackburn, P., Hasle, P., & Øhrstrøm, P.(Eds.),. (2019). *Logic and philosophy of time: Further themes from Prior, volume 2*. Aalborg University Press.

Blackburn, P., de Rijke, M., & Venema, Y. (2001). *Modal logic*. Cambridge University Press.

Bolc, L., & Szałas, A.(Eds.),. (1995). *Time and logic: A computational approach*. University College London.

Braüner, T. (2011). *Hybrid logic and its proof-theory*. Springer.

Braüner, T., Øhrstrøm, P., & Hasle, P. (2000). Determinism and the origins of temporal logic. In *Advances in temporal logic* (pp. 185–206). Springer.

Braüner, T. (2022). Hybrid logic. In E. N. Zalta (Ed.), *The Stanford encyclopedia of philosophy* (Spring 2022 ed.). Stanford, CA: Metaphysics Research Lab, Stanford University.

Bresolin, D., Della Monica, D., Goranko, V., Montanari, A., & Sciavicco, G. (2013). Metric propositional neighborhood logics on natural numbers. *Software & Systems Modeling, 12*(2), 245–64.

Broersen, J. (2011). Deontic epistemic stit logic distinguishing modes of mens rea. *Journal of Applied Logic, 9*(2), 137–52.

Brown, M. A. (2014). Worlds enough, and time: Musings on foundations. In T. Müller (Ed.), *Nuel Belnap on indeterminism and free action*, (pp. 99–121). Springer.

Bull, R. (1970). An approach to tense logic I. *Theoria, 36*(3), 282–300.

Burgess, J. (1978). The unreal future. *Theoria, 44*(3), 157–79.

Burgess, J. (1979). Logic and time. *Journal of Symbolic Logic, 44*(4), 566–82.

Burgess, J. (1980). Decidability for branching time. *Studia logica, 39*(2–3), 203–18.

Burgess, J. (1982a). Axioms for tense logic: II. Time periods. *Notre Dame Journal of Formal Logic, 23*(4), 375–83.

Burgess, J. (1982b). Axioms for tense logic: I. "'Since" and "Until"'. *Notre Dame Journal of Formal Logic, 23*(4), 367–74.

Burgess, J. (1984). Basic tense logic. In *Handbook of philosophical logic* (pp. 89–133). Springer.

Burgess, J. (2002). Basic tense logic. In D. Gabbay & F. Guenthner (Eds.), *Handbook of philosophical logic* (Vol. 7, pp. 1–43). Springer.

Burgess, J., & Gurevich, Y. (1985). The decision problem for linear temporal logic. *Notre Dame Journal of Formal Logic, 26*(2), 115–28.

Carnielli, W., & Coniglio, M. E. (2020). Combining logics. In E. N. Zalta (Ed.), *The Stanford encyclopedia of philosophy* (Fall 2020 ed.). Stanford, CA: Metaphysics Research Lab, Stanford University.

Cocchiarella, N. B. (2002). Philosophical perspectives on quantification in tense and modal logic. In D. Gabbay & F. Guenthner (Eds.), *Handbook of philosophical logic* (Vol 7, pp. 672–713). Springer.

Conradie, W., Marais, C., & Goranko, V. (2023). *Axiomatisations of some classes of trees in the Priorean temporal language.* In preparation.

Copeland, B. J. (2022). Arthur Prior. In E. N. Zalta (Ed.), *The Stanford encyclopedia of philosophy* (Summer 2022 ed.). Stanford, CA: Metaphysics Research Lab, Stanford University.

Correia, F., & Iacona, A. (Eds.). (2013). *Around the tree: Semantic and metaphysical issues concerning branching and the open future* (Vol. 361). Springer.

Dean, T. L., & McDermott, D. V. (1987). Temporal database management. *Artificial Intelligence, 32*(1), 1–55.

Della Monica, D., Goranko, V., Montanari, A., & Sciavicco, G. (2011). Interval temporal logics: A journey. *Bulletin of EATCS, 3*(105), 73–99.

Demri, S., Goranko, V., & Lange, M. (2016). *Temporal logics in computer science.* Cambridge University Press.

Dyke, H., & Bardon, A. (Eds.). (2013). *A companion to the philosophy of time* (Vol. 154). John Wiley & Sons.

Emerson, E. (1990). Temporal and modal logics. In J. van Leeuwen (Ed.), *Handbook of theoretical computer science* (Vol. B, pp. 995–1072). MIT Press.

Emerson, E. A., & Clarke, E. M. (1982). Using branching time temporal logic to synthesize synchronization skeletons. *Science of Computer Programming, 2*(3), 241–66.

Emerson, E. A., & Halpern, J. Y. (1985). Decision procedures and expressiveness in the temporal logic of branching time. *Journal of computer and system sciences, 30*, 1–24.

Emerson, E., & Sistla, A. (1984). Deciding full branching time logic. *Information and Control*, *61*, 175–201.

Emery, N., Markosian, N., & Sullivan, M. (2020). Time. In E. N. Zalta (Ed.), *The Stanford encyclopedia of philosophy* (Winter 2020 ed.). Stanford, CA: Metaphysics Research Lab, Stanford University.

Euzenat, J., & Montanari, A. (2005). Time granularity. In *Handbook of temporal reasoning in artificial intelligence* (pp. 59–118). Elsevier.

Fagin, R., Halpern, J. Y., Moses, Y., & Vardi, M. Y. (1995). *Reasoning about knowledge*. MIT Press.

Finger, M., & Gabbay, D. (1992). Adding a temporal dimension to a logic system. *Journal of Logic, Language and Information*, *1*, 203–33.

Finger, M., & Gabbay, D. (1996, Spring). Combining temporal logic systems. *Notre Dame Journal of Formal Logic*, *37*(2), 204–32.

Finger, M., Gabbay, D., & Reynolds, M. (2002). Advanced tense logic. In D. Gabbay & F. Guenthner (Eds.), *Handbook of philosophical logic* (Vol. 7, pp. 43–204). Springer.

Fisher, M. (2008). Temporal representation and reasoning. In F. van Harmelen, V. Lifschitz, & B. Porter (Eds.), *Handbook of knowledge representation* (pp. 513–50). Elsevier.

Fisher, M. (2011). *An introduction to practical formal methods using temporal logic*. Wiley.

Fisher, M., Gabbay, D., & Vila, L. (Eds.). (2005). *Handbook of temporal reasoning in artificial intelligence*. Elsevier.

Fitting, M. (2022). Intensional logic. In E. N. Zalta & U. Nodelman (Eds.), *The Stanford encyclopedia of philosophy* (Winter 2022 ed.). Stanford, CA: Metaphysics Research Lab, Stanford University.

Fitting, M., & Mendelsohn, R. L. (1998). *First order modal logic*. Kluwer Academic Publishers.

Florio, C. D., & Frigerio, A. (2020). The thin red line, Molinism, and the flow of time. *Journal of Logic, Language and Information*, *29*(3), 307–29. DOI: http://10.1007/s10849-019-09304-4.

Gabbay, D. (1973). A survey of decidability results for modal, tense and intermediate logics. In A. Heyting, J. Keisler, A. Moskowski, A. Robinson & P. Suppes (Eds.), *Proceedings of the fourth international congress on logic, methodology and philosophy of science* (pp. 29–43). North-Holland.

Gabbay, D. (1975). Decidability results in non-classical logics. *Annals of Mathematical Logic*, *8*, 237–95.

Gabbay, D. (1981). An irreflexivity lemma with applications to axiomatizations of conditions on linear frames. In U. Mönnich (Ed.), *Aspects of philosophical logic* (pp. 67–89). Reidel.

Gabbay, D. M. (1987). The declarative past and imperative future: Executable temporal logic for interactive systems. In B. Banieqbal, H. Barringer, & A. Pnueli (Eds.), *Temporal logic in specification, Altrincham, UK, April 8–10, 1987, Proceedings* (Vol. 398, pp. 409–48). Springer.

Gabbay, D., & Guenthner, F. (Eds.). (2002). *Handbook of philosophical logic*, (2nd ed., Vol. 7). Springer.

Gabbay, D., Hodkinson, I., & Reynolds, M. (1994). *Temporal logic, vol. 1: Mathematical foundations and computational aspects*. Clarendon Press.

Gabbay, D., Pnueli, A., Shelah, S., & Stavi, J. (1980). On the temporal analysis of fairness. In *Proceedings of POPL '80 (Proceedings of the Seventh Annual ACM Symposium on Principles of Programming)* Languages (pp. 163–73). ACM Press.

Gabbay, D., Reynolds, M., & Finger, M. (2000). *Temporal Logic, Vol. 2: Mathematical foundations and computational aspects, vol. 2* Clarendon Press.

Gabelaia, D., Kontchakov, R., Kurucz, A., Wolter, F., & Zakharyaschev, M. (2005). Combining spatial and temporal logics: Expressiveness vs. complexity. *Journal of Artificial Intelligence Research, 23*, 167–243.

Gallois, A. (2016). Identity over time. In E. N. Zalta (Ed.), *The Stanford encyclopedia of philosophy* (Winter 2016 ed.). Stanford, CA: Metaphysics Research Lab, Stanford University.

Galton, A. (1987). Temporal logic and computer science: An overview. In A. Galton (Ed.), *Temporal logics and their applications* (pp. 1–52). Academic Press.

Galton, A. (1995). Time and change for AI. In D. M. Gabbay, C. J. Hogger, J. A. Robinson, & Antony A. Galton (Eds.), *Handbook of logic in artificial intelligence and logic programming, vol. 4: Epistemic and temporal reasoning* (pp. 175–240). Oxford University Press.

Galton, A. (1996). Time and continuity in philosophy, mathematics, and artificial intelligence. *Kodikas/Code, 19*(1–2), 101–19.

Garson, J. W. (1984). Quantification in modal logic. In D. Gabbay & F. Guenthner (Eds.), *Handbook of philosophical logic, volume II: Extensions of classical logic* (Vol. 165, pp. 249–307). Reidel.

Goldblatt, R. (1992). *Logics of time and computation* (2nd ed.). CSLI.

Goranko, V. (1996). Hierarchies of modal and temporal logics with references pointers. *Journal of Logic, Language and Information, 5*, 1–24.

Goranko, V. (2016). *Logic as a tool: A guide to formal logical reasoning*. Wiley.

Goranko, V., Montanari, A., & Sciavicco, G. (2003). Propositional interval neighborhood temporal logics. *Journal of Universal Computer Science, 9*(9), 1137–67.

Goranko, V., Montanari, A., & Sciavicco, G. (2004). A road map of interval temporal logics and duration calculi. *Journal of Applied Non-Classical Logics, 14*(1–2) 9–54.

Goranko, V., & Rumberg, A. (2020). Temporal logic. In E. N. Zalta (Ed.), *The Stanford encyclopedia of philosophy* (Spring 2020 ed.). Stanford, CA: Metaphysics Research Lab, Stanford University.

Goranko, V., & Shkatov, D. (2010). Tableau-based decision procedures for logics of strategic ability in multiagent systems. *ACM Transactions on Computational Logic, 11*(1), 3–51.

Goranko, V., & van Drimmelen, G. (2006). Complete axiomatization and decidablity of Alternating-time temporal logic. *Theoretical Computer Science, 353*, 93–117.

Goré, R. (1999). Tableau methods for modal and temporal logics. In M. D'Agostino, D. Gabbay, R. Hähnle, & J. Posega (Eds.), *Handbook of tableau methods* (pp. 297–396). Kluwer.

Grädel, E., & Otto, M. (1999). On logics with two variables. *Theoretical Computer Science 224*(1–2), 73–113.

Gurevich, Y., & Shelah, S. (1985). The decision problem for branching time logic. *The Journal of Symbolic Logic, 50*, 668–81.

Halbach, V. (2010). *The logic manual.* Oxford University Press.

Halpern, J., & Shoham, Y. (1991). A propositional modal logic of time intervals. *Journal of the ACM, 38*(4), 935–62.

Halpern, J., & Vardi, M. (1989). The complexity of reasoning about knowledge and time I: Lower bounds. *Journal of Computer and System Sciences, 38*(1), 195–237.

Hamblin, C. (1972). Instants and intervals. In J. Fraser, F. Haber, & G. Mueller (Eds.), *The study of time (volume 1)* (pp. 324–31). Springer.

Hamm, F., & Bott, O. (2021). Tense and aspect. In E. N. Zalta (Ed.), *The Stanford encyclopedia of philosophy* (Fall 2021 ed.). Stanford, CA: Metaphysics Research Lab, Stanford University.

Hansen, M., & Chaochen, Z. (1997). Duration calculus: Logical foundations. *Formal Aspects of Computing, 9*, 283–330.

Hasle, P., Blackburn, P. R., & Øhrstrøm, P. (2017). *Logic and philosophy of time: Themes from Prior, volume 1.* Aalborg University Press.

Hodges, W. (2001). *Logic – an introduction to elementary logic*, 2nd edition. Penguin Books.

Hodges, W., & Johnston, S. (2017). Medieval modalities and modern methods: Avicenna and Buridan. *IfCoLog Journal of Logics and Their Applications, 4*(4), 1029–73.

Hodkinson, I., & Reynolds, M. (2007). Temporal logic. In P. Blackburn, J. Van Benthem, & F. Wolter (Eds.), *Handbook of modal logic* (Vol. 3, pp. 655–720). Elsevier.

Hodkinson, I., Wolter, F., & Zakharyaschev, M. (2000). Decidable fragment of first-order temporal logics. *Annals of Pure and Applied Logic, 106*(1–3) 85–134.

Hodkinson, I., Wolter, F., & Zakharyaschev, M. (2001). Monodic fragments of first-order temporal logics: 2000–2001 A.D. In R. Nieuwenhuis & A. Voronkov (Eds.), *Logic for programming, artificial intelligence, and reasoning* (pp. 1–23). Springer.

Hodkinson, I. M., Wolter, F., & Zakharyaschev, M. (2002). Decidable and undecidable fragments of first-order branching temporal logics. In *17th IEEE symposium on Logic in Computer Science (LICS 2002), 22–25 July 2002, Copenhagen, Denmark, Proceedings* (pp. 393–402). IEEE Computer Society.

Humberstone, I. L. (1979). Interval semantics for tense logic: Some remarks. *Journal of Philosophical Logic, 8,* 171–196.

Humberstone, L. (2016). *Philosophical applications of modal logic.* College Publications.

Ju, F., Grilletti, G., & Goranko, V. (2018). A logic for temporal conditionals and a solution to the sea battle puzzle. In G. Bezhanishvili, G. D'Agostino, G. Metcalfe, & T. Studer (Eds.), *Proceedings of the 12th International Conference on Advances in Modal Logic (AiML' 2018)* (pp. 407–426). College Publications.

Kamp, H. (1971). Formal Properties of 'Now'. *Theoria, 37,* 227–73.

Kamp, H. (1979). Events, Instants and Temporal Reference. In R. Bäuerle, U. Egli, & C. Schwarze (Eds.), *Semantics from different points of view* (pp. 376–417). De Gruyter.

Kamp, H., & Reyle, U. (1993). *From discourse to logic: Introduction to modeltheoretic semantics of natural language, formal logic and discourse representation theory.* Kluwer Academic Publishers.

Kamp, J. (1968). *Tense logic and the theory of linear order* (Doctoral dissertation UCLA). UCLA ProQuest Dissertations Publishing.

Kesten, Y., & Pnueli, A. (2002). Complete proof system for QPTL. *Journal of Logic and Computation, 12*(5), 701–45.

Kontchakov, R., Kurucz, A., Wolter, F., & Zakharyaschev, M. (2007). Spatial logic + temporal logic=? In M. Aiello, J. Van Benthem, & I. Pratt-Hartmann (Eds.), *Handbook of spatial logics* (pp. 497–564). Springer.

Kontchakov, R., Lutz, C., Wolter, F., & Zakharyaschev, M. (2004). Temporalising tableaux. *Studia Logica, 76*(1), 91–134.

Kowalski, R., & Sergot, M. (1986). A logic-based calculus of events. *New Generation Computing*, *4*(1), 67–95.

Koymans, R. (1990). Specifying real-time properties with metric temporal logic. *Real Time Systems*, *2*(4), 255–299.

Kröger, F., & Merz, S. (2008). *Temporal logic and state systems*. Springer.

Kuhn, S. T., & Portner, P. (2002). Tense and time. In D. Gabbay & F. Guenthner (Eds.), *Handbook of philosophical logic* (pp. 277–346). Springer.

Kurucz, A., Wolter, F., Zakharyaschev, M., & Gabbay, D. (2003). *Multidimensional modal logics: Theory and applications*. Elsevier.

Ladkin, P. (1987). *The logic of time representation* (Unpublished doctoral dissertation). University of California, Berkeley.

Lamport, L. (1994, March). The temporal logic of actions. *ACM Transactions on Programming Languages and Systems*, *16*(3), 872–923.

Lindström, S., & Segerberg, K. (2007). Modal logic and philosophy. In P. Blackburn, J. van Benthem, & F. Wolter (Eds.), *Handbook of modal logic* (Vol. 3, pp. 1149–1214). North-Holland.

Linsky, B., & Zalta, E. N. (1994). In defense of the simplest quantified modal logic. *Philosophical Perspectives*, *8*, 431–458.

Lorini, E. (2013). Temporal logic and its application to normative reasoning. *Journal of Applied Non-Classical Logics*, *23*(4), 372–399.

Ludlow, P. (2021). Descriptions. In E. N. Zalta (Ed.), *The Stanford encyclopedia of philosophy* (Fall 2021 ed.). Metaphysics Research Lab, Stanford University.

Lutz, C., Wolter, F., & Zakharyaschev, M. (2008). Temporal description logics: A survey. In S.P. Demri & C. S. Jensen (Eds.), *2008 15th International Symposium on Representation and Reasoning* (pp. 3–14). IEEE Computer Society.

Manna, Z., & Pnueli, A. (1992). *The temporal logic of reactive and concurrent systems: Specifications*. Springer.

Marx, M., & Reynolds, M. (1999). Undecidability of compass logic. *Journal of Logic and Computation*, *9*(6), 897–914.

McArthur, R. P. (1976). *Tense logic* (1st ed., Vol. 111). D. Reidel Publishing Company.

McCall, S. (1994). *A model of the universe: Space-time, probability, and decision*. Oxford University Press.

McCarthy, J., & Hayes, P. J. (1969). Some philosophical problems from the standpoint of artificial intelligence. In B. Meltzer & D. Michie (Eds.), *Machine intelligence 4* (pp. 463–502). Edinburgh University Press.

McDermott, D. (1982). A temporal logic for reasoning about processes and plans. *Cognitive Science, 6*(2), April, 101–55.

Merz, S. (1992). Decidability and incompleteness results for first-order temporal logics of linear time. *Journal of Applied Non-Classical Logics, 2*(2), 139–56.

Meyer, U. (2013). *The nature of time.* Oxford University Press.

Meyer, U. (2015). Tense Logic. *Philosophy Compass, 10*(6), 406–19.

Montanari, A. (1996). *Metric and layered temporal logic for time granularity* (Doctoral dissertation, ILLC, University of Amsterdam). ILLC Dissertation Series, 1996-02.

Montanari, A., & Policriti, A. (1996). Decidability results for metric and layered temporal logics. *Notre Dame Journal of Formal Logic, 37*(2), 260—82.

Moszkowski, B. (1983). *Reasoning about digital circuits* (Doctoral dissertation, Department of Computer Science, Stanford University, Stanford, CA). Technical Report STAN-CS-83-970.

Müller, T. (Ed.). (2014). *Nuel Belnap on indeterminism and free action* (Vol. 2). Springer.

Nishimura, H. (1979). Is the semantics of branching structures adequate for chronological modal logics? *Journal of Philosophical Logic, 8*(4), 469–75.

Øhrstrøm, P. (2014). What William of Ockham and Luis de Molina would have said to Nuel Belnap: A discussion of some arguments against 'the Thin Red Line'. In T. Müller (Ed.), *Nuel Belnap on indeterminism and free action* (Vol. 2, pp. 175–190). Springer.

Øhrstrøm, P. (2019). A critical discussion of Prior's philosophical and tense-logical analysis of the ideas of indeterminism and human freedom. *Synthese, 196*(1), 69–85.

Øhrstrøm, P., & Hasle, P. (2006). Modern temporal logic: The philosophical background. In *Handbook of the history of logic* (Vol. 7, pp. 447–98). Elsevier.

Øhrstrøm, P., & Hasle, P. (2020). Future Contingents. In E. N. Zalta (Ed.), *The Stanford encyclopedia of philosophy* (Summer 2020 ed.). Metaphysics Research Lab, Stanford University.

Øhrstrøm, P., & Hasle, P. F. V. (1995). *Temporal logic: From ancient ideas to artificial intelligence.* Springer.

Pani, A., & Bhattacharjee, G. (2001). Temporal representation and reasoning in artificial Intelligence: A review. *Mathematical and Computer Modelling, 34*(1–2), 55–80.

Pinto, J., & Reiter, R. (1995). Reasoning about time in the situation calculus. *Annals of Mathematics and Artificial Intelligence, 14*(2), 251–68.

Ploug, T., & Øhrstrøm, P. (2012). Branching time, indeterminism and tense logic. *Synthese, 188*(3), 367–79.

Pnueli, A. (1977). The temporal logic of programs. In *Proceedings of the Eighteenth IEEE Symposium on the Foundations of Computer Science* (pp. 46–57). IEEE Computer Society.

Prior, A. N. (1957). *Time and modality.* Clarendon Press.

Prior, A. N. (1962). Tense logic and the continuity of time. *Studia Logica, 13,* 133–48.

Prior, A. N. (1967). *Past, present and future.* Oxford University Press.

Prior, A. N. (1968). *Papers on time and tense.* University of Oxford Press.

Reichenbach, H. (1947). *Elements of symbolic logic.* Macmillan.

Rescher, N., & Urquhart, A. (1971). *Temporal logic.* Springer.

Reynolds, M. (1994). Axiomatizing U and S over integer time. In D. Gabbay & H. J. Ohlbach (Eds.), *Proceedings of the first International conference on temporal logic* (pp. 117–32). Springer-Verlag.

Reynolds, M. (1996). Axiomatising first-order temporal logic: Until and Since over linear time. *Studia Logica, 57*(2/3), 279–302.

Reynolds, M. (2001). An axiomatization of full computation tree logic. *The Journal of Symbolic Logic, 66*(3), 1011–57.

Reynolds, M. (2002). Axioms for Branching Time. *Journal of Logic and Computation, 12*(4), 679–97.

Reynolds, M. (2003). An Axiomatization of Prior's Ockhamist logic of historical necessity. In P. Balbiani, N. Y. Suzuki, F. Wolter, & M. Zakharyaschev (Eds.), *Proceedings of AiML 2002* (pp. 355–70).

Reynolds, M. (2005). An axiomatization of PCTL *. *Information and Computation, 201*(1), 72–119.

Reynolds, M. (2007). A tableau for bundled CTL*. *Journal of Logic and Computation, 17*(1), 117–32.

Reynolds, M. (2010). The complexity of temporal logic over the reals. *Annals of Pure and Applied Logic, 161*(8), 1063–96.

Reynolds, M. (2011). A tableau-based decision procedure for CTL*. *Formal Aspects of Computing, 23*(6), 739–79.

Reynolds, M. (2014). A Tableau for temporal logic over the reals. In R. Goré, B. Kooi, & A. Kurucz (Eds.), *Advances in modal logic* (vol. 10, pp. 439–58). CSLI Publications.

Reynolds, M., & French, T. (2003). A sound and complete proof system for QPTL. In P. Balbiani, N. Y. Suzuki, F. Wolter, & M. Zakharyaschev (Eds.), *Advances In modal logic* (pp. 127–48). King's College Publications.

Röper, P. (1980). Intervals and tenses. *Journal of Philosophical Logic, 9*(4), 451–69.

Rumberg, A. (2016). Transition semantics for branching time. *Journal of Logic, Language and Information, 25*(1), 77–108.

Santelli, A. (Ed.). (2022). *Ockhamism and philosophy of time*. Springer.

Segerberg, K. (1970). Modal logics with linear alternative relations. *Theoria, 36*(3), 301–22.

Sistla, A., & Clarke, E. M. (1985). The complexity of propositional linear temporal logics. *Journal of the ACM, 32*(3), 733–49.

Steedman, M. (1997). Temporality. In J. van Benthem & A. ter Meulen (Eds.), *Handbook of logic and language* (pp. 895–938). Elsevier.

Stirling, C. (1992). Modal and temporal logics. In *Handbook of logic in computer science* (Vol. 2, Background: Computational Structures), pp. 477–563). Clarendon Press.

ter Meulen, A. (2005). Temporal reasoning in natural language. In M. Fisher & D. Gabbay (Eds.), *Handbook of temporal logic In artificial intelligence*, vol. 1 (pp. 559–86). Elsevier.

Thomason, R. (1970). Indeterminist time and truth-value gaps. *Theoria, 36*(3), 264–81.

Thomason, R. (1984). Combinations of tense and modality. In D. Gabbay & F. Guenthner (Eds.), *Handbook of philosophical logic, volume II: Extensions of classical logic* (pp. 135–166). Reidel.

Uckelman, S. L. (in press). *Modal logic*. Cambridge University Press.

Uckelman, S. L., & Uckelman, J. (2007). Modal and temporal logics for abstract space–time structures. *Studies in History and Philosophy of Science Part B: Studies in History and Philosophy of Modern Physics, 38*(3), 673–81.

van Benthem, J. (2010). *Modal logic for open minds*. CSLI Publications.

van Benthem, J. (1983). *The logic of time – a model-theoretic investigation into the varieties of temporal ontology and temporal discourse* (Vol. 156). Springer.

van Benthem, J. (1995). Temporal logic. In D. Gabbay, C. J. Hogger, & J. A. Robinson Eds.), *Handbook of logic in artificial intelligence and logic programming* (pp. 241–350). Oxford: Clarendon Press.

van Benthem, J., & Pacuit, E. (2006). The tree of knowledge in action: Towards a common perspective. In G. Governatori, I. M. Hodkinson, & Y. Venema (Eds.), *Proceedings of Advances in Modal Logic, 2006* (pp. 87–106). College Publications.

Vardi, M. Y. (2007). Automata-theoretic techniques for temporal reasoning. In P. Blackburn, J. Van Benthem, & F. Wolter (Eds.), *Handbook of modal logic* (Vol. 3, pp. 971–89). Elsevier.

Venema, Y. (1990). Expressiveness and completeness of an interval tense logic. *Notre Dame Journal of Formal Logic, 31*(4), 529–47.

Venema, Y. (1991). A modal logic for chopping intervals. *Journal of Logic and Computation, 1*(4), 453–76.

Venema, Y. (1993). Completeness via Completeness: Since and Until. In M. de Rijke (Ed.), *Diamonds and defaults* (pp. 279–86). Kluwer.

Venema, Y. (2001). Temporal logic. In L. Goble (Ed.), *The Blackwell Guide to Philosophical Logic* (pp. 259–81). Wiley-Blackwell.

Vila, L. (1994). A survey on temporal reasoning in artificial intelligence. *AI Communications, 7*(1), 4–28.

Wałęga, P. (2019). Hybrid fragments of Halpern-Shoham logic and their expressive power. *Theoretical Computer Science, 797*, 102–28.

Walker, A. G. (1947). Durées et instants. *Revue Scientifique, 131*–34.

Wölfl, S. (1999). Combinations of tense and modality for predicate logic. *Journal of Philosophical Logic, 28*(4), 371–98.

Wolper, P. (1985). The tableau method for temporal logic: An overview. *Logique et Analyse, 110–111*, 119–36.

Wolter, F., & Zakharyaschev, M. (2000). Temporalizing description logics. In D. Gabbay & M. de Rijke (Eds.), *Frontiers of combining systems 2* (Vol. 2, pp. 379–402). Research Studies Press.

Wolter, F., & Zakharyaschev, M. (2002). Axiomatizing the monodic fragment of first-order temporal logic. *Annals of Pure and Applied Logic, 118*(1–2) 133–45.

Xu, M. (1988). On some U, S-tense logics. *Journal of Philosophical Logic,* 181–202.

Zanardo, A. (1985). A finite axiomatization of the set of strongly valid Ockamist formulas. *Journal of Philosophical Logic, 14*, 447–68.

Zanardo, A. (1990). Axiomatization of 'Peircean' branching-time logic. *Studia Logica, 49*(2), 183–95.

Zanardo, A. (1991). A complete deductive system for since-until branching time logic. *Journal of Philosophical Logic, 20*, 131–48.

Zanardo, A. (1996). Branching-time logic with quantification over branches: The point of view of modal logic. *Journal of Symbolic Logic, 61*(1), 1–39.

Zanardo, A. (1998). Undivided and indistinguishable histories in branching time logics. *Journal of Logic, Language and Information, 7*, 297–315.

Zanardo, A., Barcellan, B., & Reynolds, M. (1999). Non-definability of the class of complete bundled trees. *Logic Journal of the IGPL, 7*(1), 125–36.

Øhrstrøm, P., & Hasle, P. (2020). Future contingents. In E. N. Zalta (Ed.), *The Stanford encyclopedia of philosophy* (Summer 2020 ed.). Metaphysics Research Lab, Stanford University.

Acknowledgements

For numerous helpful comments, suggestions, and corrections on drafts of this Element, I am grateful to Johan van Benthem, Torben Braüner, Mark Brown, Melvin Fitting, Dov Gabbay, Dimitar Guelev, Fengkui Ju, Przemysław Wałęga, and Alberto Zanardo, as well as the anonymous reviewers. (I am particularly indebted to Mark and Przemysław for their meticulous reading of the submitted draft of this Element and, besides making useful comments on the content, also correcting a great many language and typographic glitches.) I thank Angelo Montanari and Guido Sciavicco for their kind permission to include in the book some figures from our previous joint publications.

I also acknowledge the encouragement, advice, and support of the Cambridge University Press Elements in Philosophy and Logic series editors Bradley Armour-Garb and Frederick Kroon, as well as the contribution of Antje Rumberg for comprehensive corrections and editing done on my parts of the text of the *Stanford Encyclopedia of Philosophy* article Goranko and Rumberg (2020), from which the present Element evolved.

Lastly, I thank my partner Nina for her help and support during my work on this text.

Cambridge Elements ☰

Philosophy and Logic

Bradley Armour-Garb

SUNY Albany

Brad Armour-Garb is chair and Professor of Philosophy at SUNY Albany. His books include *The Law of Non-Contradiction* (co-edited with Graham Priest and J. C. Beall, 2004), *Deflationary Truth* and *Deflationism and Paradox* (both co-edited with J. C. Beall, 2005), *Pretense and Pathology* (with James Woodbridge, Cambridge University Press, 2015), *Reflections on the Liar* (2017), and *Fictionalism in Philosophy* (co-edited with Fred Kroon, 2020).

Frederick Kroon

The University of Auckland

Frederick Kroon is Emeritus Professor of Philosophy at the University of Auckland. He has authored numerous papers in formal and philosophical logic, ethics, philosophy of language, and metaphysics, and is the author of *A Critical Introduction to Fictionalism* (with Stuart Brock and Jonathan McKeown-Green, 2018).

About the Series

This Cambridge Elements series provides an extensive overview of the many and varied connections between philosophy and logic. Distinguished authors provide an up-to-date summary of the results of current research in their fields and give their own take on what they believe are the most significant debates influencing research, drawing original conclusions.

Cambridge Elements ≡

Philosophy and Logic

Printed in the United States
by Baker & Taylor Publisher Services